REGIONAL CO-OPERATION
IN ASIA

LIBRARY
OVERSEAS DEVELOPMENT INSTITUTE
111 WESTMINSTER BRIDGE ROAD
LONDON SE1 7JD, UK
TEL: +44(0)20 7922 0300
FAX: +44(0)20 7922 0399
Email: odi@odi.org.uk
Website: www.odi.org.uk

The **Japan Institute of International Affairs** (JIIA) is a private, non-profit, and independent research organization founded in 1959 through the initiative of former Prime Minister Shigeru Yoshida, the first president of the JIIA.

The JIIA's mission is to contribute to the formulation of Japan's foreign policy through organizing study groups on regional and global issues, international conferences, symposiums and seminars, and joint research projects with other domestic and overseas research organizations and universities. The JIIA also invites foreign researchers to Japan and assists them with their research activities, and it issues a wide range of publications as a result of these activities.

The **ASEAN Foundation** was established by ASEAN leaders in 1997 to boost ASEAN's effort to promote region's co-operation in various fields of social and human development such as science and technology, youth, women, health and nutrition, education, labour affairs, disaster management, HIV/AIDS prevention and control, children, population, and rural development and poverty eradication, culture and information, environment, drug matters, and civil service. The Foundation was established to promote greater awareness of ASEAN, greater interaction among the peoples of ASEAN as well as their wider participation in ASEAN activities.

The ASEAN Foundation deems that the most beneficial and effective means to attain its objectives is focusing on human resources development projects such as education, training, seminars, workshops, exchanges, network-building, fellowships and information dissemination.

The **Institute of Southeast Asian Studies (ISEAS)** was established as an autonomous organization in 1968. It is a regional centre dedicated to the study of socio-political, security and economic trends and developments in Southeast Asia and its wider geostrategic and economic environment.

The Institute's research programmes are the Regional Economic Studies (RES, including ASEAN and APEC), Regional Strategic and Political Studies (RSPS), and Regional Social and Cultural Studies (RSCS).

ISEAS Publications, an established academic press, has issued more than 1,000 books and journals. It is the largest scholarly publisher of research about Southeast Asia from within the region. ISEAS Publications works with many other academic and trade publishers and distributors to disseminate important research and analyses from and about Southeast Asia to the rest of the world.

Asian Development Experience Vol 3

REGIONAL CO-OPERATION IN ASIA

Edited by

Ryokichi Hirono

JAPAN INSTITUTE OF INTERNATIONAL AFFAIRS

ASEAN FOUNDATION

LSEAS

INSTITUTE OF SOUTHEAST ASIAN STUDIES, Singapore

First published in Singapore in 2003 by
Institute of Southeast Asian Studies
30 Heng Mui Keng Terrace
Pasir Panjang
Singapore 119614
http://bookshop.iseas.edu.sg

All rights reserved. No part of this publication may be reproduced, stored
in a retrieval system, or transmitted in any form or by any means,
electronic, mechancial, photocopying, recording or otherwise, without
the prior permission of the Institute of Southeast Asian Studies, the JIIA
and the ASEAN Foundation.

© 2003 Japan Institute of International Affairs and ASEAN Foundation

*The responsibility for facts and opinions expressed in this publication rests
exclusively with the authors whose interpretations do not necessarily reflect the
views or the policy of ISEAS.*

ISEAS Library Cataloguing-in-Publication Data

Asian Development Experience. Volume 3, Regional Co-operation in Asia
  / edited by Ryokichi Hirono.
  1. Regionalism—Asia, Southeastern.
  2. Regionalism—Asia.
  3. Japan—Relations—Asia, Southeastern.
  4. Asia, Southeastern—Relation—Japan.
  5. Japan—Relation—Asia.
  6. Asia, Southeastern—Relation—Japan.
  I. Hirono, Ryokichi.
  II. Title: Regional Co-operation in Asia
HC412 A865 v. 3   2003

ISBN 981-230-204-2 (soft cover)
ISBN 981-230-201-8 (hard cover)

Printed in Singapore by Utopia Press Pte Ltd
Typeset by International Typesetters Pte Ltd

Contents

List of Tables

List of Figures

Contributors

Ryokichi HIRONO is Professor Emeritus at Seikei University, Japan

Hank LIM is Director for Research at the Singapore Institute of International Affairs, Singapore

Deunden NIKOMBORIRAK is a Research Fellow at the Thailand Development Research Institute, Thailand

Hadi SOESASTRO is the Executive Director at the Centre for Strategic and International Studies, Indonesia

Somkiat TANGKITVANICH is a Research Fellow at the Thailand Development Research Institute, Thailand

Gwendolyn R. TECSON is Professor at the School of Economics of the University of the Philippines, Philippines

Acknowledgements

This volume owes much to the efforts and patience of many people including the authors themselves and the organizations associated with a two-year research project, "Asian Development Experience", organized by the Japan Institute of International Affairs (JIIA). Unfortunately, SARS, which became widespread in East Asia in particular, prevented the holding of an interim workshop scheduled for April 2003.

Thanks are due to Matsuo Watanabe and Saori Honma of JIIA who facilitated the progress of the project since its inauguration in November 2001, as well as to the the Japan-ASEAN Solidarity Fund, contributed by the Japanese Government and managed by the ASEAN Foundation, whose financial support made the project possible. A special thanks goes to Hisashi Owada, former president of JIIA, now judge in the International Court of Justice in the Hague, Netherlands, who inaugurated the launch meeting of the project in Tokyo.

1

Structural Changes and Domestic Reforms in Singapore: Challenges and Implications to Regional Co-operation in ASEAN and East Asia

Hank Lim

1. Structural Shift in Global and Regional Environment

Singapore's remarkable economic transformation in the last four decades has been, to a large extent, due to its capacity to leverage on external sources and external markets to achieve economic output far beyond its domestic production possibility curve. Such sterling policy performance was the result of far-sighted policy makers in managing and optimizing emerging favourable external environments. Specifically, the Government provided world-class infrastructure, transparent and effective institutions and sound macroeconomic policy framework to create economic value for the global marketplace. As a result, Singapore has been one of the favourite investment destinations for multinational companies in this part of the world.

Lately, there have been several major events occurring in the global and regional environments that have serious long-term implications to Singapore's economic viability and performance. Firstly, the Asian financial and economic crisis in 1997 has devastated the financial and real sectors of many Southeast Asian economies that serve as Singapore's hinterland for resources and market. The quick economic recovery in ASEAN and in Singapore in 2000 was primarily due to export expansion from low export bases and stimulus from highly devalued regional currencies. It would take many years for the ASEAN economies to fully recover from the debilitating financial sector mismanagement and non-performing loans in the financial and banking sector. As a regional hub, Singapore cannot prosper as long as the regional hinterland remains economically weak, and socially and politically instable. Singapore needs a prosperous and dynamic Southeast Asia to complement it in an environment of competitive regional clustering.

The second major external change is the accelerating market liberalization and borderless nature of the global economy. The global marketplace has become strikingly more competitive and more complex as a result of this relentless process of global production networking. The new global economic structure, widely known as the New Economy, is the product of three major elements, namely, information technology, changes in government policy and corporate restructuring. Information technology is an important force shaping the contours of the global economy and contributing to the shortening of the product cycle and changes in the comparative and competitive advantage of trading countries. The shift to information technology as the basis for industrial production is forcing a change in industrial organizations. Economic globalization, together with the IT revolution, is undermining the competitiveness of the large, vertically integrated industrial organizations that have been the mainstays of the East Asian industry in the age of industrial technology. Networking organizations that utilize out-sourcing and supply-chain management are more suited to the new IT environment than self-contained organizations.

As a result of this IT revolution, the comparative advantage of many industrial economies, including Singapore, is affected by this new configuration of industrial location. With the process of globalization and IT revolution, the "flying geese" model is becoming less relevant to describe the pattern of development in East Asia. Differences in the adaptability of East Asian economies to these external changes are disturbing the pattern and distribution of industrial locations in East Asia.

The third major external factor is the accession of China to the World Trade Organization (WTO) in November 2001. When China acceded to the WTO, ASEAN countries were alarmed by the prospect of a head-to-head competition for trade and investment with China. Even before becoming a formal member, China had been enjoying the Most Favoured Nations (MFN) benefits accorded by the US and EU on a year-to-year basis. However, after the formal accession, China now has to abide by the binding commitments and responsibilities on liberalization and de-regulation of its largely closed domestic economy. On the other hand, China is assured of market access to the world's richest industrial economies and accorded full privileges as a member of the WTO.

To take advantage of China's huge domestic market and more transparent domestic economic policies, the flow of foreign direct investment (FDI) has been directed to China, even before China officially became a WTO member. In the early 1990s, ASEAN economies received almost two-thirds more of FDI than China. During 2000–2001, China received more than double in FDI than ASEAN economies. This is a drastic reversal of FDI flows within a decade. It is expected that China's trade competitiveness would continue to increase against ASEAN export products, especially in labour-intensive and mid-range industrial output.

2. Domestic Implications to External Challenges

Global economy in a borderless context leads to radical changes in economic structures. Distinct economic entities become subsumed into the global system by international processes and transactions. National economies and business organizations are significantly affected and transformed by the process of globalization. In turn, this process causes radical changes in the production process, in which prices are brought down and production shifts from high-cost to low-cost locations. Specifically, such processes exert pressures that bring about changes in the product market and work practices, in productivity and in the demand for and supply of labour. Globalization and information technology cause major structural changes across domestic industrial sectors. Companies are re-structuring to make the best use of global resources, and re-engineering job processes to harness new technologies. Mergers and acquisitions in corporate businesses, shortening product cycles and new knowledge-intensive industries are changing macro- and microeconomic landscapes.

Globalization, liberalization and de-regulation are affecting large and small economies in the developed and developing economies at differing levels and degrees. For a small and open economy such as Singapore, the pace and extent of changes on the domestic economy could be de-stabilizing if it is not managed properly and quickly. The Asian financial crisis in 1997 heightened Singapore's awareness that it had become less competitive as compared to other economies in the region where currencies had devalued sharply. Cost-cutting measures in existing industries are short-term measures. Industrial upgrading was hampered by Singapore's relative lack in indigenous technology base and skilled workforce and other capabilities generally identified in developed economies. In an increasingly challenging global environment characterized by intensified global competition and rapid technological change, and facing skill, resource and domestic market constraints, Singapore must tap new sources of economic growth to maintain its competitive edge.

The current challenge facing Singapore is that of transforming into a knowledge-based economy (KBE). To become a KBE, Singapore will need human and intellectual capital to create, absorb, process and apply knowledge, a strong technological capability and an entrepreneurial culture. To realize this vision requires a quantum leap in capabilities. Domestic constraints on growth and a rapidly changing external environment have forced Singapore, a small and highly open city-state, to restructure its economy more frequently and dramatically than larger and less open economies. Sources of growth in the future would increasingly come from knowledge-based economic activities such as research and development, innovation, product and service design, process and marketing in the real and financial sectors for the local, regional and global marketplace. At the same time, rapid and large changes in the process of creating and producing income necessitate equally large changes in the labour market, social safety nets, Central Provident Fund (CPF), the role of government and the government-linked companies and small and medium enterprises.

2.1 Changes in the Labour Market

The transition from pre-industrial to post-industrial stage of development involves disequilibrium process and major changes both in the product and factor markets. Many OECD (Organisation for Economic Co-operation and Development) countries are also experiencing a continous shift in their industrial structures. Some were able to make adjustments without causing much dislocation in their domestic economies. With sound long-term planning, and flexible and effective management of industrial and labour policies, an economy would be able to make a smooth transition without causing industrial hollowing and structural unemployment. The basic problem of these adjustment policies is due to the divergence of the rate of technological growth on one hand, and social and institutional changes on the other. Often social and institutional structures, especially in a democratic society, are not able to keep pace with rapidly changing production technologies. As a result, many necessary adjustment policies are implemented suboptimally and are inconsistent with market demands and specifications. This is particularly critical for a small and open economy devoid of natural resources, and dependent on external markets and leveraging, on external high-grade manpower to generate its economic growth.

Like other industrialized economies, Singapore's industrial structure has shifted to the service sector as there is a limit to how much the manufacturing sector can expand. The emergence of KBE and borderless production frontiers are causing industrial restructuring and dislocation in the product and factor markets. New skills are required and many traditional industrial sectors are in danger of decline or relocation to other production bases, where technology-based industries are established. The basic problem is that the propensity of the rate of decline of the established industries is much higher than the rate of increase of new industries (bio-chemical industries).

The nature of work, the range of occupations and the skill requirements are rapidly changing. The growth of the Singapore economy will greatly depend upon the qualitative improvement rather than the quantitative expansion of its labour force. In this context, the level of educational qualifications of the labour force is another major policy issue. The percentage of workers with tertiary qualifications is still low compared to that of other advanced industrial countries.

Theoretically, the demand for labour in Singapore is determined exogenously. Since the industrial sector is dominated by electronic, electrical, computer peripherals, machinery, petroleum and petrochemical products, the patterns of labour demand have been very much determined by the changing demand for these products in the world marketplace. Therefore, the demand for labour has been determined by structural changes in the economy and the rapid shift of demand for labour in the high-productivity sector. As a result, the demand for labour has shifted dramatically in favour of highly skilled labour. It has become more apparent in the labour market that changes in demand would not be met by changes in supply due to emerging discrepancy in the demand for and supply of different categories of workers.

The increase in foreign workers' participation rate in the domestic labour force has raised concern over the loss of job opportunities and suppressed wages, particularly with respect to lower skilled workers. When full employment was attained in the early 1970s, Singapore had increasingly relied on the import of skilled and unskilled foreign labour to make up for the shortfall in the domestic labour supply. In recent years, the focus has shifted toward building a critical mass of knowledge workers to address the skills shortage in knowledge-intensive growth industries. As a result, foreign skilled labour's contribution to quarterly GDP growth has increased significantly to a high of 36.9% during the period of Q1 1991–Q4 2000.

For the Singapore economy to remain competitive internationally, domestic labour has to be willing to adapt to changing economic conditions. Other than the emphasis on lifelong learning and the need to 'top-up' the local talent pool with multinational talent, domestic labour also faces new labour practices such as variable wages through monthly variable wage component and profitsharing. Increasingly, employment will tend to be on short-term contract basis for firms to reduce fixed costs and to increase the variable component of production costs.

2.2 Restructuring the Domestic Sector

In the early stage of development, Singapore lacked private entrepreneurship and capital in many sectors of the economy. There was an urgent need to structure our economy from one based on import substitution to that of export-oriented industrialization. This was done through foreign capital, market and technology. To complement and balance the presence of multinational companies (MNCs) and to speed up the process of industrial development, a number of government-linked companies (GLCs) were established to spearhead development in specific strategic and key sectors of the economy such as shipbuilding, transport, shipping and development banking.

Over the years, the GLCs have accumulated technical expertise and proven track record in public sector operations and infrastructural development. The GLCs were estimated to have contributed 12.9% of Singapore's GDP in 1998. While this was substantially lower than what was widely perceived, it was not insignificant: amounting to more than a quarter of local-controlled companies' estimated contribution of 46% to GDP. Furthermore, with 11 GLCs making the list of the top 30 largest companies in Singapore, their dominance over private enterprises in the domestic economy is apparent.

The question now arises as to whether these GLCs have outgrown their original purpose of catalyzing industrialization and economic development. Harvard economist, Professor Michael Porter, and other economists argue that Singapore's next stage of development as an advanced economy will have to be innovation-led, spearheaded by strong private sector companies. The private sector needs to spread its wings and develop itself in order to take a leading role in Singapore's next lap of development.

The economic rationale in establishing government-linked companies is to create competitive, viable and efficient business organizations that can compete in the local, regional and world marketplace. This is particularly crucial since the Singapore economy is small, open and dominated by large multinational companies. Small and medium enterprises (SMEs) are viewed as another vital element required for a viable and resilient, small open economy.

In theory, GLCs are established on the same basis as the private companies–without receiving preferential treatment from the Government. However, in practice, the line between GLCs and the public sector is difficult to differentiate. This is due to the fact that many key and senior civil servants are involved in one form or another in the management of the GLCs. In addition, due to the size of their capital bases and multifaceted operations, the GLCs are able to benefit from economies of scale much more than the SMEs. As a result, local SMEs are at a disadvantage and cannot develop to their full potential as envisaged by the Government.

In the past, when the Singapore's economy was growing rapidly, the urgency and significance of a robust private sector and enhanced SMEs were not acutely felt by the policy makers. To a large extent, the basic issues of growth and employment creation remained anchored in promoting vibrant external growth impulses. Currently, the Singapore economy is experiencing a cyclical downturn and structural imbalances. The electronic and computer peripherals sector is at a cyclical downturn phase. A slow-paced emergence of new sources of growth in knowledge-based industries and some contradictions existing in the domestic economy have been worsened by the 911 terrorists attack on the US, and the accession of China to the WTO. In responding to these challenges, the Government has established a high-level Economic Review Committee to examine some of the existing fundamental policy paradigms, and established assumptions of long-held economic practices. The role and relevancy of GLCs and the enhanced role of the SMEs are being re-examined in view of the rapidly changing global and regional challenges.

It is generally agreed that GLCs remain relevant and have a strategic role to play in the emerging knowledge-based economy driven by knowledge, enterprise, and innovation provided by the private sector and spearheaded by the GLCs. Such an approach would synergise the relative strength of the private sector and the GLCs.

SMEs, which make up 90% of business establishments and 50% of employment, are a vital part of the Singapore economy. However, their contribution to the Singapore economy is hampered by their poor productivity performance. The Productivity and Standard Board (PSB) has been tasked as the lead agency to develop vibrant and resilient SMEs that will enhance Singapore's competitiveness and economic growth.

The Strategic Economic Plan (SEP) drawn up by the Economic Planning Committee provided an overview of the economic landscape over the next two to three decades. The SEP called for the promotion and development of Singapore as a 'total business centre' through the development of high-tech and high-value added manufacturing and services as twin engines of growth. It made two strategic proposals: 1) for Singapore to evolve into a highly developed manufacturing and service cluster; and 2) upgrade the low productivity domestic sector. The cluster proposal adopted Michael Porter's framework for competitiveness that business enterprises need access to various suppliers, competency centres in relevant technologies, efficient infrastructure and other services.

The key thrusts of the SEP are to develop an international orientation, to maintain international competitiveness, to develop manufacturing and service clusters, and to develop a climate conducive to innovation, to enhance human resources and to reduce economic vulnerability. These strategies are grouped under Manufacturing 2000 (M2000) and International Business Hub 2000 programmes.

The strategic goal is to sustain manufacturing at 25% of Gross National Income (GNP) and at 20% of national employment. These targets were slightly below the sector's share in the first half of the 1990s. The model for Singapore's continued role as a manufacturing base is value chain analysis in which modern manufacturing and services act as integrated and complementary activities. In this view, industrial capacity is an essential component of any advanced industrial economy, providing the foundation for building advanced capabilities in science and technology and operations management.

The key element of M2000 is the development of industry clusters. The programme has specific actions plans for major sectors, including electronics. The strategy is to upgrade capabilities across the value chain in each industry cluster, including product and process development, production, engineering and strategic marketing.

The International Business Hub 2000 programme focused on strategies to develop Singapore into a hub for business and finance, logistics and distribution, communication and information. The basis of this hub strategy is the concept that key economic activities such as finance, shipping, air transport, telecommunications, and information are becoming concentrated into a few strategic nodes around the world. Each node acts as a hub providing services to be extended hinterland and linking it with the rest of the world. In this regard, Singapore aims to have the first mover advantage as the business hub in the region in leveraging its competitive advantage as regional trading, financial, transport and telecommunication centres from its strategic location and also to have well-developed infrastructure, institutions and human resources.

As the regional economies industrialized, the entrepôt trade shifted from a two-way exchange of the primary products of Southeast Asian economies for western manufactures to a two-way trade in manufactures and intra-industry trade. Following the recommendations of the Competitiveness Report, the Economic Development Board (EDB) launched Industry 21, a 10-year plan to develop Singapore into a vibrant and robust global hub of knowledge-driven industries in manufacturing and traded services with emphasis on technology, innovation and capabilities. Industry 21 identified electronics, chemicals, engineering, life sciences, education and healthcare, headquarters, communications, media and logistics as industry clusters to be nurtured.

Supporting the EDB's work to achieve the goals of Industry 21, the International Enterprise (IE) Singapore is promoting and marketing Singapore's total trade capabilities through its trade regulation, facilitation and promotion functions. The IE facilitates Singapore to leverage its advantage in information technology and position itself as a centre for e-business.

Currently, Singapore's economy is in the process of economic structural adjustment. The basic problem is not the magnitude of slow growth and the rate of unemployment, but the existence of internal distortions and inconsistencies of policies brought about by the rapidly changing external factors. Domestic political, social and economic expediency, however, do not justify the implementation of rapid policy changes in savings, housing, the role of government, Central Provident Fund (CPF), labour, and social safety nets. Therefore, a certain fine-tuning and policy balancing with respect to the level and speed of adjustment are required to maintain an element of continuity and change in the social and economic policies.

The source of economic growth has been shifting from factor-based to knowledge-based and accelerated through information, communication and technology (ICT) revolution. These external changes, as manifested through globalization, have brought about drastic changes in the mode of production and consumption in developed and developing economies. But for a small and open economy like Singapore, the required changes must be planned and implemented well in advance before they become structural problems. Singapore does not have much policy leverage and room to manoeuvre in the face of rapid external shocks and changes.

In the end, economic policies that worked well in the past based on the premise of rapid economic growth and full employment, may not be functioning in the future.

3. Regional Pattern of Development

Prior to the Asian financial crisis in 1997, there were already visible economic indicators pointing to the strain and stress of export-led growth– the existence of poor public and corporate governance, import-inducing industrial structures and inadequate human resource development in some ASEAN countries. Domestic low total factor productivity, fixed exchange rate regime and other inadequacies were compounded with over-borrowing from external sources which ultimately led to the financial collapse in Thailand and its contagion effect throughout the East Asian economies. Due to the strict and rigid rules of the International Monetary Fund (IMF) on lending, Thailand, Indonesia and Korea that borrowed heavily from the IMF had to reduce subsidies and public spending. Reduced aggregate spending in the real sector led to a full-blown economic crisis first in those debt-ridden and ultimately, through regional interdependence in trade and investment, the rest of the East Asian economies were seriously affected in one form or other.

The Asian economic crisis marked a major turning point in the East Asian economies. Some argue that the East Asian economic 'miracle' has turned to a 'mirage'. Most of the East Asian economies had recovered in the year 2000 basically due to export-led recovery, but their economic recovery is based on narrow economic fundamentals. Most of the crisis-affected ASEAN economies, especially Indonesia and to some extent Thailand and the Philippines, have not been able to restructure their debt-ridden financial and banking sector due to their external debts and industrial structure that were too dependent on import contents. Even Singapore and Malaysia are facing serious economic challenges to widen their industrial base and to upgrade their industrial structure to higher value-added and knowledge-based economy.

On the other hand, after the Asian economic crisis, China emerged relatively unscathed and continued its rapid and dynamic economic growth, especially after its entry into the WTO in November 2001. During the period of 2001–2002, two thirds of foreign direct investment (FDI) to East Asia had been invested in China and one third went to ASEAN countries, a dramatic reversal of FDI flow as compared to the early 1990s. China is now the pre-eminent economic 'engine of growth' and the driver of the East Asian economies. Notwithstanding China's enormous domestic economic challenges and adjustments it has to make after its entry into the WTO, most analysts predict that China would overcome its transitional restructuring problems.

Korea was devastated due to the Asian financial crisis, but under the strong political leadership of President Kim Dae-Jung, it has made headway in restructuring its financial and banking sector and reorganizing its highly concentrated industrial structure known as *chaebols*. As a result, the Korean economy has gradually reformed to become more competitive and productive in its real and financial sectors.

The Taiwan and Hong Kong economies are currently having economic maladjustment problems because of the rapid shifting of economic comparative advantage in favour of China. Many manufacturing industries have been shifting their operations to China because of the much lower cost of production and much larger domestic market. During this transition period, the two economies would have structural problems but in the long-run both Taiwan and Hong Kong are expected to be able to upgrade their economies because of their sound economic fundamentals and enormous financial resources to finance their transitional difficulties.

Japan, being the second largest industrial economy in the world, and the most technologically developed in East Asia would play a critical role in the development of Northeast and Southeast Asian economies. If Japan channels its FDI to China, Korea, Taiwan and Hong Kong, then the East Asian economic divide would widen. On the other hand, as the Japanese national interests would dictate, Japan spreads its FDI to ASEAN as well as to Northeast Asian economies, the possible regional economic divide would be minimized. To continue as an attractive investment destination, ASEAN needs urgently to embark on domestic restructuring and a more cohesive regional co-operation with the effective implementation of ASEAN Free Trade Area (AFTA), AFTA–Plus,

ASEAN Investment Area (AIA) and ASEAN Free Trade Agreement on Trade in Services (AFAS).

In the past, the development pattern of East Asia has been described as the 'flying-geese' pattern. It implies that there was a leader and a group of countries following the leader at different levels of growth. Japan started the East Asian growth path as the first-tier industrial economy in East Asia. Following Japan were Korea, Taiwan, Hong Kong and Singapore as the second tier economies to transform their economies from developing to the developed status. The third tier were the ASEAN countries of Thailand, Malaysia, Indonesia and the Philippines. As a result of this regional interdependence through investment and trade, there was a regional cycle of economic band that linked all Northeast and Southeast Asian economies into a dynamic and sustainable growth pattern for more than two decades.

In the aftermath of the Asian economic crisis, the process of globalization and the information and communication technology (ICT) revolution, the 'flying-geese' of economic development has become less relevant. Differences in the adaptability of the East Asian economies to embark on economic restructuring, responding to challenges posed by globalization and information technology disturbed the previous order of regional development.

Theoretically, the 'flying -geese' pattern of industrial development in East Asia has two characteristics: the traditional sequential development of individual 'full-set' industrial structures and the recent development of cross-border production networks through FDI. With the closer integration of the world economies, the full-set component is losing significance and the network component is becoming dominant.

The development pattern emerging in East Asia seems to be one in which regional clusters form around each new technological breakthrough. There are clusters of production-oriented around technology involving economies at different stages of development. There is no longer a single economy that leads the whole flock but different leaders for each technology cluster. For example, Korea leads Japan in the production of random-access memory (RAM) chips and Taiwan excels in the production of PCs and China in the mass-based labour and capital-intensive production.

The regional pattern of network-based development driven by FDI and the application of IT depends on the comparative advantage of each economy. Differences in comparative advantage tend to support a sequential 'flying-geese' pattern of development, as industrial change accumulates through time and is orderly. On the other hand, differences in competitive advantage other than comparative advantage do not generate an obvious, predictable pattern of development. These differences arise from many factors such as market and regulatory framework, taxation, infrastructure, the development of industrial clusters, and the externalities of international networks.

The competitive advantage of an economy is increasingly influenced by the choice of policies and their implementation as well as by the networking activities of corporations, rather than mere factor endowments as were the case in the past. This emerging reality is a wake-up call for most ASEAN economies. If ASEAN economies are not able to upgrade their public and corporate governance to make policy choices more transparent, predictable and effective, their comparative advantage in factor endowments would constitute much less of economic value. It is therefore vital for ASEAN governments to make their domestic economic regime and policy implementation more effective and reduce the accompanying transaction costs in producing goods and services.

Specifically, Thailand, Indonesia, the Philippines and to some extent Malaysia must reorganize and restructure their public and corporate governance, human resource development and financial and banking sector. Domestic reforms can be more conveniently implemented and politically feasible when their economies are growing fast. On the other hand, without enhanced regional co-operation to implement those agreed liberalization and de-regulation policies, ASEAN economies seem to be stuck to an unsustainable growth not so much due to their own inertia but due to the dynamic competitive forces of China, Northeast Asian economies and other rapidly growing emerging economies in other parts of the world. Market forces and rapid technological development on the global and regional levels would tend to increase the economic gap between Northeast and Southeast Asian economies.

The East Asian economies need to be reorganized and restructured to meet the challenges of globalization, IT revolution, regionalization and production networking. To compete in such environment, these economies need to have a flexible and productive labour force, good public and corporate governance and industrial structures that reflect the importance of information technology and the decline of mechanical technology. This paradigm shift in the production mode and system is driving structural changes in East Asian industries.

First of all, the paradigm shift is accelerating the transfer of mature industrial technology of manufacturing from advanced to less-developed economies in the region. The prospect of establishing competitive advantage based on lower costs gives a firm incentive to transfer mature production technologies through FDI. For example, the flood of Japanese investments into Southeast Asia and China followed by the newly industrialized economies (NIEs) investment in the region since the middle of 1980s reflected this process. Second, the shift from industrial to information technology increased the share of the IT industries in the economies of East Asia. The IT industry's share of GDP in Korea, Taiwan, Hong Kong and some ASEAN economies is increasing at different rates. Third, the shift to information technology increases the knowledge content of the production process as information substitutes for labour and capital in the production process. This is readily seen in the increasing demand for knowledge workers in the rapidly growing IT investment in developed economies. Changes in the production process requirement may put a premium on innovation capability at the expense of knowledge-absorption capability in which East Asian countries excelled in the past.

In addition, the shift to information technology as the basis for industrial production is forcing a change in industrial organizations. Economic globalization and the IT revolution are reducing the competitiveness of the large, vertically integrated industrial organizations that have been the mainstays of East Asian industries in the past. Networking organizations that utilize outsourcing and supply-chain management are more suited to the new IT environment than self-contained organizations such as *chaebols*, *keiretsu* and many industrial conglomerates in ASEAN countries.

Other major fundamental changes are in the area of liberalization and de-regulation. These measures are intended to enhance industrial efficiency by eliminating distortions in the allocation of resources. However, liberalization and de-regulation have not been implemented in all economic sectors of East Asia uniformly, particularly in ASEAN. Throughout the region, the service sector remains protected and less competitive than the manufacturing sector. The reform of state-owned enterprises (SOEs) and the development of the private sector are central to China's ability to realize its transformation into a productive market-based economy. State monopolies are prevalent in Thailand, Indonesia, Malaysia and the Philippines, even in Singapore with the prevalence of government-linked companies (GLCs). The slow pace of regulatory reform in Japan and Korea has undermined the international competitiveness of the Japanese and Korean industries by keeping them from improving innovative capacity and efficiency.

The Asian financial crisis has had a strong impact on the liberalization and regulatory reform in the crisis-hit economies. The crisis seemed to have significantly accelerated the trend of liberalization in those economies but its implementation is slow due to slow economic growth and the lack of structural reforms. On the other hand, the Asian economic crisis has caused some backlashes against continued liberalization. Slow growth in the economy has induced political and social instability in Indonesia, an anchor of ASEAN which in turn has caused uncertainty about the ASEAN Free Trade Area (AFTA) and other agreed regional co-operation schemes. The liberalization policy has recently slowed down in the Philippines with the imposition of limits on inward FDI to the air transport and petroleum industries. Malaysia has requested for a deferment on the free trade status of automobile imports until 2005 in order to protect its national car industry. The different approaches and ways that East Asian economies adjust their liberalization policies may give rise to differences in industrial efficiency and international competitiveness.

Many of these elements of competitive advantage can be shaped by government policies by developing a physical and regulatory infrastructure and by subsidizing investments to enhance these policy-dependent competitive factors. The ability of government policies to raise the skill and knowledge base of their high-grade labour resources will determine which activities these economies can attract and the shape of their industrial structures.

4. Regional Economic Co-operation and Integration

4.1 Singapore's Trade Policy

Because of the rapidly changing external and internal environment facing East Asian economies, governments in the region are looking for ways and means to enhance regional economic co-operation on regional and bilateral framework. In the past, the multilateral approach to trade and investment liberalization has been the prime policy objective of economies in the region. They relied on the General Agreement on Tariffs and Trade (GATT)/WTO principles of Most-Favoured Nations (MFA) clause and non-discrimination to liberalize trade and investment. However, with the rising regional economic integration in North America and in Europe and the slow down in the WTO multilateral process, East Asian governments started to look inward and resorted to regional and bilateral approaches in liberalizing trade and investment regimes.

The successful conclusion of the WTO Ministerial Meeting in Doha to launch the 'Development Round' in November 2001, and the full implementation of AFTA in January 2003, do not provide an adequate liberalization impetus to small and open economy such as Singapore. Accordingly, Singapore started initiating bilateral free trade areas (FTA) with like-minded economies with a policy objective to supplement and strengthen the regional and multilateral frameworks. The agreement between New Zealand and Singapore on a Closer Economic Partnership (ANZSCEP) was the first FTA Singapore concluded after the AFTA. Although New Zealand is not Singapore's major trading partner, but its perceived benefits are to set off a further impetus for bilateral agreement with Australia since New Zealand and Australia have a Closer Economic Relations and Trade Agreement (ANCERTA). Following the FTA agreement with New Zealand, Singapore initiated bilateral negotiations with Australia,

Japan, the US, European Union, European Free Trade Area (EFTA), and a trilateral trade negotiation among Singapore, Chile and New Zealand.

The Japan–Singapore Economic Partnership Agreement (JSEPA) was concluded in January 2002. The JSEPA is a landmark trade agreement for Japan that covers elements of free trade area and a comprehensive agreement on other economic aspects such as technical and educational, information and communication technology, co-operation and liberalization in service trade. This agreement is a major departure from the Japanese established multilateral approach on trade liberalization.

Following the JSEPA, agreements on the free trade area were reached with European Free Trade Area (EFTA) in 2002, the US in January and Australia in February 2003 respectively. The FTA agreement with the US (USSFTA) has special elements to include integrated Production Outsourcing Scheme. This scheme is an innovative trade arrangement whereby the US has agreed to include the Indonesian islands of Batam and Bintan to receive free import duty privileges on their exports of electronic and computer peripheral equipments to the US. The objective is to widen the trade and investment space of Singapore and at the same time to encourage investment flows to the two adjacent Indonesian islands. Special reference should be made that the USSFTA is very comprehensive and ambitious in that both the US and Singapore have agreed way above their WTO commitments. It will be a NAFTA-plus in a number of areas such as intellectual property protection, the inclusion of e-commerce, ICT services, local content requirements (source of origin) and custom co-operation. Other Singapore bilateral trade initiatives with Canada, Mexico and Korea are at different stages of negotiations.

Singapore's efforts to initiate and negotiate FTAs with its major trading partners have drawn criticism from other ASEAN members. Initially, Malaysia and other ASEAN members expressed that Singapore had violated the AFTA agreement with respect to local content requirements. However, Singapore maintained that its bilateral FTA met strict requirements of AFTA and was consistent with articles 5 and 24 of the WTO.

Recent development indicates that the other ASEAN members are also interested in initiating bilateral FTAs with Japan and the US. Thailand and the Philippines, even Malaysia have indicated their interest on the bilateral approach to trade liberalization. It is not critical whether it is on the basis of bilateral, regional or multilateral approach, as long as it is directed toward the ultimate objective of freer and more transparent movement of goods, services and investments across national borders. For that matter, the WTO and the multilateral trading system remain the ultimate objective of Singapore. It is the fundamental trade policy of Singapore to ensure that global trade is premised on the rule-based multilateral trading system where goods, services and investments flow freely with minimum impediment.

4.2 ASEAN–China FTA

After one year of intensive discussions and a study on China's proposal to initiate a free trade area with ASEAN, the leaders of ASEAN and China signed a 'Framework Agreement on Comprehensive Economic Co-operation between ASEAN and China' on 4 November 2002 in Phnom Penh. The agreement goes beyond and explicitly aims at the establishment of an ASEAN–Free Trade Area (FTA) within 10 years. This initiative is of major economic and political significance to both ASEAN and China and has taken the Japanese Government by surprise. The negotiations, conducted by the ASEAN–China Trade Negotiation Committee will produce schedules for tariff reductions and eliminations from 1 January 2005 to 2010 for ASEAN and China and from January 2005 to 2015 for the newer members of ASEAN.

The accession of China into the WTO as the seventh largest world exporter would have significant impact on the global and regional trading system. The most important impact will be felt in the domestic economy as it has to abide by the liberalization and de-regulation policies of its largely closed domestic economy. On the other hand, China's exports are accorded protection under the WTO's most-favoured-nations clause. Accession into the WTO will bring challenges and opportunities to China, the region and the world. Liberalizing the Chinese economy will increase its efficiency and at the same time, put tremendous competitive pressure on domestic firms, state-owned enterprises (SOEs) which will lead to increased unemployment and large-scale industrial dislocation. If China can manage to register at least 6–7% of annual economic growth in the transitional period, in the long-run, China would benefit enormously from the process of liberalization and de-regulation following its entry into the WTO. The critical point is in the transition period where China must have adequate economic growth in order to minimize the expected large-scale unemployment and industrial dislocation of SOEs because of intense foreign competition and liberalization of domestic market in the real and financial sectors.

Against these external and internal challenges, the former Prime Minister Zhu Ronji of China took a bold policy initiative to propose ASEAN–China FTA within 10 years. An FTA with ASEAN would provide policy leverage and economic space for China to embark on its domestic reforms and liberalization, especially in the early period. China is expected to gain competitive advantage against ASEAN in the early period due to its rapidly growing economic momentum while ASEAN remains straddled in the slow growth path. During the period of 2001–2002, China received two-thirds of FDI to East Asia while ASEAN received one-third, a complete reversal of the FDI data as compared to the early 1990s.

From the start of negotiations, China was more interested and prepared in negotiating the issues and agenda for an FTA. This could be due to the fact that China is represented by a single entity while ASEAN composes of 10 members with diverse interests and preferences. Among the ASEAN-6 (Singapore, Malaysia, Thailand, Brunei, the Philippines and Indonesia), there are a wide range of views and differing political, economic and social configurations and priorities. This inertia may be the reason why ASEAN economies are growing much slower and less dynamic when compared to China. As a result, ASEAN's negotiating posture has been more reactive rather than proactive in identifying opportunities in the FTA negotiating process with China.

The ASEAN–China Agreement explicitly spells out that the agreement is not strictly an FTA but involves a comprehensive economic co-operation. If it is a strict FTA, the negotiation would be protracted and it would be difficult to reach a trade-off or consensus because negotiating an FTA alone would be too narrow. It would be more difficult to strike a win-win scenario for both sides. Therefore, the scope of ASEAN–China FTA had to be broad and contain trade, facilitation and development objectives, rather than just focus on trade liberalization negotiated by the Trade Negotiating Committee of ASEAN and China.

Basically, the economies of ASEAN and China are less complementary but more competitive because both are producing similar products across a broad range of labour intensive and mid-term range, capital-intensive industrial goods. Even if the scope is wide, there is a possibility that there might be a delay or to yield a "dirty ASEAN–China FTA" if economic growth and macroeconomic conditions in ASEAN and China are not substantively expanding during the period of negotiations. For example, if ASEAN fails to attract sufficient FDI because of the lack in domestic economic reforms or if there are large-scale unemployment or serious structural dislocation in China arising from opening its domestic market, the FTA negotiations can be seriously disrupted.

The ASEAN–China FTA is based on the assumption that East Asia regional co-operation will bring greater benefits to the region as it involves a larger grouping, division of labour, economies of scale and clustering. It is likely that in the initial period China may gain relatively more than ASEAN but China is ready to recycle the economic benefits to ASEAN countries through larger outflow of FDI, tourism and import of ASEAN agro-related industrial goods and other services. In the long run, trade creations and intra-regional investment flows would generate positive income effects to offset the initial period of negative substitution effects.

Many ASEAN countries fear the ominous competition that China poses to their own economies. China is a large continental economy of 1.3 billion, has a large domestic market, highly skilled workforce that is low-priced and relative political stability compared to ASEAN. Moreover, the economic and export structures of ASEAN and China are generally similar in products lines and export destinations. There is a lingering fear that the low-priced Chinese products may flood the Southeast Asian markets. With its differential regions and levels of skill, the Chinese workforce is understood to be able to churn out the full spectrum of products from textiles to electronics, cameras and refrigerators. On the other hand, ASEAN countries have no viable alternative but to promote greater regional co-operation and integration in the hope that this regional mechanism would provide vital growth impulses for their domestic economies and added impetus for further liberalization and restructuring.

To overcome this initial structural incompatibility, China has offered to ASEAN a set of 'early harvest' benefits. This implies that while China offers preferential tariffs to ASEAN exports in agriculture-related products in the early period of negotiation, there is no reciprocal treatment of China's exports to ASEAN, particularly to the CMLV (Cambodia, Myanmar, Laos and Vietnam) countries. In addition, it is also important that the ASEAN–China FTA negotiations should not be entirely left to both sides of the Trade Negotiating Committee in order to minimize administrative delay. Both sides must bring in strong political support to include developmental elements in the negotiation and endorsement from the highest political leadership. Otherwise, the negotiation process would be bogged down with unnecessary impediments resulting in a diluted or less optimal outcome for both ASEAN and China.

4.3 ASEAN–Japan Comprehensive Economic Partnership

To balance China's bold FTA initiative, ASEAN and Japanese leaders have agreed to initiate ASEAN–Japan Comprehensive Economic Partnership (AJCEP) at the ASEAN + 3 Summit in Phnom Penh in November 2002. In contrast with the ACFTA, the AJCEP is at its initial stage and lacks details and programme of implementation.

In terms of economic structure, ASEAN and Japan are complementary. ASEAN is rich in natural resources while Japan is rich in technology and investment capital. However, the Japanese economy is saddled with many restrictions and non-competitive economic practices, such as high tariffs and quotas on rice and other agricultural products and many forms of trade impediments in the Japanese domestic sector. Due to these structural impediments in the Japanese economy, it is not possible to negotiate a standard free trade area. A comprehensive economic partnership (CEP) structure provides a broad range of issues to be discussed and negotiated including an element of free trade area between ASEAN and Japan. Theoretically, CEP allows sufficient negotiating space for Japan and the diverse economic interest of ASEAN economies.

In the past, Japan adopted a multilateral approach, having considered that regional and bilateral were suboptimal approach to its international trade policy. The breakthrough came when Japan and Singapore concluded the Japan–Singapore Economic Partnership Agreement (JSEPA) in January 2002 that came into effect in November 2002. JSEPA not only covers tariff cuts but movement of people, the rules of investment and a broad range of technical co-operation between the two countries.

Since comprehensive economic partnership arrangement is not strictly a free trade area, its scope is not clearly defined by a standard model. Therefore, the scope and structure of the AJCEP would have to be carefully studied to identify the lowest common denominators for both sides to expedite the process of negotiation. Theoretically, the scope must be broad enough to allow sufficient negotiation space for Japan and the diverse economic interest of the ASEAN economies, taking into account the comparative advantage of each side. Interestingly, the concurrent negotiation process with ACFTA would definitely provide a strategic forward thrust for the AJCEP and a healthy competition that would provide a strong impetus for the realization of a wider vision of East Asia economic community in the long run.

As AJCEP is being negotiated, Japan is also undertaking bilateral FTA with individual ASEAN economies. Thailand, Malaysia and the Philippines have indicated an interest to enter bilateral FTA negotiations with Japan. Therefore, Japan has to ensure that the bilateral trade policy approach is consistent with the regional framework in order to minimize the 'spaghetti bowl syndrome' in the East Asian region. There is an indication that Japan is giving more preference to bilateral trading arrangement with ASEAN-6 at the expense of new ASEAN members since it is based on the interplay of market forces. ASEAN-6 is economically more important to Japan than Cambodia, Myanmar, Laos and Vietnam.

The success of the AJCEP is highly dependent on the Japan's strong interest and capacity to assist ASEAN industrial upgrading and competitiveness. After the Asian financial crisis, it became acutely evident that many ASEAN economies require major structural reorganization and upgrading. Without these changes in the real and financial sectors, ASEAN economies would not be able to take full advantage of a comprehensive economic partnership with Japan. Foreign direct investment has been radically shifting in favour of China and the gravity of economic dynamism and growth have contributed to the widening economic gap between Northeast Asian and ASEAN countries.

In order to reverse or balance this trend, Japan has to extend substantive technical and financial assistance to ASEAN countries with a view to radically reorganize and restructure their economies. Specifically, ASEAN countries need to upgrade the quality of their labour force and infrastructure with respect to administrative and governance in the public and private sectors.

It is imperative and vital for ASEAN to retain and attract FDI as sources of economic growth. Without increasing supply of FDI and other forms of capital, there would be more social and political instability. Thus, creating a more difficult domestic constituency to accept further trade and investment liberalization and regional economic integration. In turn, a viable and vibrant ASEAN would enable it to have the capacity to be the critical hub to connect intrinsically rivalling economic power of China and Japan. Stability and balance between the two Northeast Asian economic and political powers are indeed preconditions for the establishment of a prosperous and peaceful East Asia and the realization of the East Asian Economic Community.

4.4 The Role of Japan

Being the world's second largest economy, the vitality of the Japanese economy is very important to the economic growth of East Asia. Since 1993, Japan has been experiencing economic problems characterized as structural maladjustment resulting in slow growth and three recessions in the past 10 years. This is due to asset deflation and the existence of huge non-performing loans that crippled the financial and banking sectors and the inability of aggregate demand to induce economic growth. Weaknesses in the economy are compounded with seemingly lack of political stewardship to lead Japan out of the economic recession. Without a revitalized Japanese economy, it is much more difficult to generate dynamic economic impulses that would translate into sustainable growth in East Asia.

Despite having slow or no growth in the past decade, Japan is by far the largest economy in East Asia. It is three to four times larger than China. Since the Asian financial crisis, China has been growing very rapidly and it serves as the engine of growth in East Asia. However, the rate and the magnitude of the Chinese economy to a large extent are influenced by the flow of Japanese Official Development Assistance (ODA), the private sector FDI and technology transfer. Equally, ASEAN economies are dependent on the flow of capital and technology from Japan to ASEAN countries. On a mid-term perspective, China would be very much occupied with domestic economic and social problems. It is the responsibility of Japan to energize and revitalize the regional economies. Japan can be a catalyst for the economic resurgence of East Asia because it has the technology and industrial capital. It is a moot whether Japan can act as the regional leader but in a minimal capacity, it has economic and industrial capacity to transform the

East Asian economies. At the same time, the economic recovery and dynamism of East Asia would provide an effective mechanism for a sustainable Japanese economic recovery at home. It is indeed a win-win formula for Japan and the region. The problem is to identify the modality and mechanism whereby critical regional economic impulses can be magnified for the benefit of ASEAN countries, China, Japan and Korea as integral constituents of the East Asian Economic Community.

The ASEAN + 3 Framework (Chiang Mai initiative) is an important mechanism to bring together Northeast and Southeast Asian countries. Under this framework, East Asian countries have learned the habit of working together for the common benefit of the region. Specifically, a regional currency swapping scheme and other financial co-operation agreements have been implemented under this framework. Japan has been an active and important contributor promoting closer financial and monetary co-operation between Northeast and ASEAN countries. Recent initiative to promote ASEAN bond market has been strongly supported by the Japanese government.

Studies have shown that East Asian regional co-operation will bring greater benefits to East Asian countries as it involves a larger grouping to offset diversionary effects of other regional trade arrangement (RTAs). Theoretically, ASEAN + 3 framework should be more preferable than a series of ASEAN + 1 arrangements. However, in practice it would be difficult to achieve, given the very diverse economic interest and structural differences among the ASEAN economies. Although the ASEAN + 1 framework is less optimal and there is a risk of overlapping arrangements, it appears that this framework is more feasible than the ASEAN + 3.

Another important aspect of the ASEAN + 1 framework is the central position of ASEAN as being the 'hub' of East Asia. ASEAN may gain this position more so by default rather than having the intrinsic virtue or power over China, Japan or Korea. The reason is simply because none of the Northeast Asian countries can gain a leadership position and a sub-regional structure would not emerge in Northeast Asia in the foreseeable future.

In this respect, Japan can play a very important role to support ASEAN as a 'hub' for closer East Asian economic co-operation. Failure to do so will allow the stronger Northeast Asian countries to dictate the terms of regional arrangement and there is a risk that ASEAN would not be supportive to further closer regional co-operation.

ASEAN must have a single overall framework that is designed by ASEAN and individual ASEAN members can negotiate bilaterally with China, Japan and Korea on the basis of a region-wide framework.

4.5 ASEAN Economic Community

At the recent ASEAN summit in November 2002 in Cambodia, ASEAN leaders agreed to explore the possibility of transforming ASEAN into an ASEAN Economic Community (AEC) by the year 2020. Although the concept of an AEC and how this would be achieved were not elaborated during the summit, it would undoubtedly involve fostering closer economic co-operation and expediting the current economic integration process. The proposed AEC could provide the means for ASEAN to revitalize and remain competitive in the face of rising challenges from globalization.

It would also stand to benefit from the global trend in trade liberalization and manufacturing by creating an attractive regional production base.

There is already an ASEAN Vision 2020 (Hanoi Plan of Action) that was agreed in 1998 which among other things, envisages an economically integrated ASEAN. The AEC would therefore assist in realizing this vision and provide a framework to achieve its economic objectives. It is a blueprint to economically integrate all ten ASEAN member countries.

ASEAN is already working toward eliminating the intra-regional trade restrictions in goods, services and investment with the aim of achieving the ASEAN Vision 2020. ASEAN could first strive for the total removal of barriers on goods among ASEAN-6 countries, followed by the removal of barriers on services and capital. Other members can join in as and when they are ready. The recently adopted 'ASEAN minus X principle' could be used to expedite the integration process. Given the wide economic disparities among the ASEAN countries, free mobility will be the longer-term objective.

Therefore, AEC would provide a comprehensive framework to build on existing ASEAN economic integration programmes such as the ASEAN Free Trade Area (AFTA), the ASEAN Framework Agreement on Services and the ASEAN Investment Area (AIA). The proposed AEC will provide an applicable road map to strengthen ASEAN's effectiveness in trade and investment creation, and in dealing with growing interdependence in all ASEAN economies. Intra-ASEAN trade now accounts for nearly a quarter of ASEAN's total trade.

The ASEAN Economic Community proposal is being discussed and debated among ASEAN Senior Officials for further submission to ASEAN Economic Ministers and Foreign Ministers. During the ASEAN Heads of Government Meeting in Bali in October 2003, ASEAN leaders will decide on the proposal, its structure, modality and mechanism for further action.

5. Conclusion

Rapid changes in international and regional environment have necessitated drastic policy and structural changes among East Asian economies. These external changes have been induced by radical changes in information and communication technology and liberalization and de-regulation of trade and investment policy regimes. As a result of these external and internal changes, established industrial structures and production patterns in the world and in East Asia have considerably changed. Competition has become much keener and product cycles have been shortened. Mature and developed economies in the region have to continually upgrade and restructure. Otherwise, these economies would be outperformed by emerging economies through changes in the division of labour and shifting comparative advantage. With the entry of China into the WTO, China provides tremendous challenges and opportunities to other East Asian economies. Arising from the prospect of strong competition from China and of more dynamic market interplay, regional free trade proposals were initiated between ASEAN and China and between ASEAN and Japan. Alternatively, free trade area and comprehensive economic partnership and co-operation can be interpreted as policy-induced measures to maximize the potential benefits and to reduce the potential negative implications of globalization and liberalization in trade and investment.

Japan can play a critical role in upgrading the ASEAN economies. In this respect, Japan should strongly support the establishment of the ASEAN Economic Community as a logical step toward closer and effective economic co-operation in ASEAN. In turn, more competitive ASEAN economies would contribute toward the East Asian Economic Community by providing the 'hub' to connect the potentially rivalling competition for leadership in East Asia between China and Japan. Stability and balance between China and Japan are vital prerequisites for a prosperous and peaceful East Asia.

2

Asia-Japan Co-operation Toward East Asian Integration

Hadi Soesastro

1. Introduction

ASEAN and Japan have played a critical, if not a pivotal, role in the establishment of regional co-operation processes in the Asia Pacific region. At the inter-governmental level the region has seen the establishment of APEC (Asia Pacific Economic Co-operation) to promote economic co-operation and the ARF (ASEAN Regional Forum) as a forum for co-operation in the political and security field to strengthen confidence building measures (CBMs). At the non-governmental level, two important "track two" processes have also emerged in the region, beginning with PECC (Pacific Economic Co-operation Council) since the early 1980s and later CSCAP (Council for Security Co-operation in the Asia Pacific). The overarching objective of these processes is to develop an Asia Pacific community.

Will ASEAN and Japan again play an important role in the creation of an East Asian community? ASEAN has made the first step toward this end by initiating the ASEAN Plus Three (APT) process, involving the ten ASEAN countries, China, Japan and South Korea. A vision for an East Asian community has been articulated by the East Asian Vision Group (EAVG) in its report, "Towards an East Asian Community", submitted to the APT Leaders at their Fifth Summit in Brunei Darussalam in November 2001. The vision is of an East Asia that moves "from a region of nations to a bona fide regional community with shared challenges, common aspirations, and a parallel destiny". Furthermore, the report also stated that "[t]he economic field, including trade, investment, and finance, is expected to serve as the catalyst in the comprehensive community-building process".

In the field of economic co-operation, the vision is that of a progressive integration of the East Asian economy, ultimately leading to an East Asian economic community. Economic integration is to be pursued

24

through the liberalization of trade and investment, development and technological co-operation, and information technology development.

In trade, it recommended the formation of an East Asia Free Trade Area (EAFTA), and the liberalization of trade should be well ahead of the Bogor Goal set by APEC. In investment, it proposed the establishment of an East Asian Investment Area (EAIA) by expanding the Framework Agreement on ASEAN Investment Area (AIA) to cover East Asia as a whole. In the area of finance, the recommendation toward greater financial integration was to adopt a staged, two-track approach, namely for the establishment of a self-help arrangement (e.g., an East Asian Monetary Fund) and for co-ordinating a suitable exchange rate mechanism amongst countries in the region.

The EAVG has also listed the various motives for the development of an East Asian community. A great deal has been written on this. Three considerations have stood out. First, the need to establish a regional (institutional) identity, in view of the fact that the other regions (Europe and the Americas) have established or are developing their own regional arrangement. Second, the need to amplify an East Asian voice on regional and global issues, in view of East Asia's increased stakes in regional and global developments. Third, the need to promote regional peace and prosperity through co-operation, given the region's own internal dynamics.

Despite this compelling rationale, difficulties and obstacles in creating an East Asian community have also been recognized. Three problems have been identified. First, the great diversities amongst countries in the region, and especially the large gaps in levels of economic development. Second, the lack of a mechanism (and tradition) for regional co-operation in Northeast Asia. Third, the prevailing politico-security problems in the region (China–Taiwan, the Korean Peninsula, and to a much lesser extent the South China Sea).

2. The ASEAN Plus Three Processes

With the development of the ASEAN Plus Three (APT) process, it can be said that ASEAN has taken the lead in establishing the foundation for eventual East Asian economic integration. This process, as suggested by its name, is supposed to be driven by ASEAN. In fact, if ASEAN had not taken the lead, this process may not have emerged. A Japanese or Chinese initiative and leadership would have killed it. Until today the main APT meetings take place in conjunction with ASEAN meetings. Some see this as a possible obstacle to the creation of a truly East Asian regional arrangement (Jayasuriya 2000).

The APT process began as a modest undertaking. Foreign ministers from the three Northeast Asian countries initially came for an informal meeting over lunch during an ASEAN meeting. There was no specific agenda for those meetings. This process attracted the involvement of the Heads of State. The first (informal) APT Summit was held in December 1997 in Kuala Lumpur. The Asian financial crisis appears to have provided the impetus for this summit. The APT process became more serious. Although the process has been and is essentially driven by ASEAN, the agenda setting was not monopolized by ASEAN.

In the Second APT Summit in Hanoi in November 1998, Korea's President, Kim Dae-jung, made his mark by proposing the establishment of an East Asia Vision Group (EAVG) to carve out a mid- to long-term vision for the co-operation. The Third APT Summit in Manila in November 1999 was held under the banner of "East Asian Co-operation". The meeting discussed various ways to promote co-operation and to cope with the new challenges of the 21st century. APT Heads of State adopted the "Joint Statement on East Asian Co-operation" suggesting co-operative measures in various areas including security, economy, culture, and development strategy. This agreement led to the launching of a series of APT meetings of finance and economic ministers, in addition to those of foreign ministers since the year 2000.

In May 2000, at the APT Finance Ministers Meeting, discussions on the need to build a regional financial framework led to the adoption of the so-called Chiang Mai Initiative (CMI). This initiative aims at creating a network out of existing currency swap arrangements of ASEAN and bilaterally between ASEAN members and the other Three countries.

In the Fourth APT Summit in Singapore in November 2000, Chinese Prime Minister Zhu Rongji came up with suggestions that the APT should focus on the following areas of co-operation: the development of Mekong River Basin transportation and communication infrastructure, IT (information technology), human resources development, agriculture, and tourism. China also took the initiative to convene an APT agriculture and forestry ministers, and offered to host an agricultural technology and co-operation business forum. Korean President Kim Dae-jung proposed the establishment of an East Asia Study Group (EASG), consisting of officials, with the mandate to assess the recommendations of the EAVG, and from that assessment, sort out a practical number of concrete measures that should be given high priority and are relatively easy to carry out. Its other task is to explore the idea and implications of an East Asian Summit.

The Singapore Summit concluded with a public statement by Prime Minister Goh Chok Tong, highlighting the "two big ideas" that emerged from the discussion, namely, the development of institutional links between Southeast Asia and Northeast Asia, and the setting up of a working group to study the merits of an East Asian free trade and investment area. In response to suggestions of transforming the APT Summit into some kind of East Asia Summit, he recommended a gradual evolution. He noted, however, that what was important was that the leaders of the thirteen countries were starting to think as "East Asian".

At the Fifth APT Summit in Brunei Darussalam in November 2001, leaders endorsed the report by the EAVG, including the development toward an East Asian Economic Community, among other means through the creation of an East Asian Free Trade Area. However, this meeting and the agreements reached were overshadowed by China's "surprising" proposal for an ASEAN–China Free Trade Agreement. The Sixth APT Summit in Phnom Penh in November 2002 was also overshadowed by global terrorism issues as well as the signing of the Framework Agreement on ASEAN–China Comprehensive Economic Co-operation, which provides the basis for negotiating an ASEAN–China Free Trade Agreement (ACFTA). In addition, the leaders of ASEAN and Japan also issued a Joint Declaration on the Comprehensive Economic Partnership between ASEAN and Japan, which may include a FTA element.

The above development shows that the APT process appears to have moved its main attention away from financial co-operation to developing FTAs in the region, seen as building blocks for an eventual region-wide free trade area, the East Asian Free Trade Area (EAFTA). Indeed, the EAVG Report made the suggestion that the establishment of an EAFTA could be achieved by adopting a building block approach, and consolidating the existing bilateral and sub-regional FTAs in the region.

This paper begins with an examination of developments in the area of trade co-operation in East Asia and suggests broad principles that will help consolidate the various trade initiatives in the region. The subsequent section will examine developments in the area of financial co-operation, which are still wide open for further initiatives, the latest being the development of the Asian Bond Market.

3. Trade Integration or Fragmentation?

It has been speculated that the ASEAN–China initiative was largely politically motivated. Strengthening of ASEAN–China relations is indeed a critical element in the development of an East Asian community. The search for an institutional identity in East Asia, as in other regions, tends to be dominated by ideas about regional trade structures, in particular FTAs. In a region as diverse as East Asia, it will not be easy to establish a region-wide free trade arrangement. There are suggestions that perhaps such a regional arrangement can result from the development of bilateral or sub-regional trading arrangements as its building blocks. Recent initiatives to form bilateral FTAs may have been inspired by that idea.

There are various possible routes to developing an East Asian institutional identity (Soesastro 2001). One possible route is through the formation of a Northeast Asian sub-regional FTA that subsequently could be linked to the one already in existence in Southeast Asia (AFTA), resulting in an East Asian Free Trade Area (EAFTA). A modified version of this is to extend AFTA's CEPT (Common Effective Preferential Tariffs) to the other Three. The other option, focussing on development co-operation, is to develop an OECD–type institution. This will require large resources to establish and to operate, and takes away much of the limelight from the political leaders. This option is a desirable one but not likely to be pursued in East Asia.

Still another route, as will be examined later, is through financial co-operation. The route that is currently being taken, namely along the pragmatic, develop-as-you-go approach, is perhaps the politically preferred one. However, there needs to be a clear vision and strategy as to how the APT process can be strengthened by the bilateral initiatives.

The ASEAN–China agreement and the ASEAN–Japan initiative will now take the centrestage. A great deal of energy and attention will be devoted by the ASEAN bureaucracies to these initiatives. ASEAN will effectively become a "hub". In September 2002, a Joint Ministerial Declaration on Closer Economic Partnership (CEP) was signed between ASEAN and the CER countries (Australia and New Zealand). In late October 2002, at the APEC meeting in Mexico, President Bush also proposed the "Enterprise for ASEAN Initiatives" that will provide a framework for the US to negotiate both bilateral and regional free trade agreements with Southeast Asia. At the First ASEAN–India Summit in November 2002, India too has offered to start free trade talks and to have a free trade agreement (FTA) working within 10 years. Australia has also courted ASEAN to have an ASEAN–Australia Summit.

Can one conclude that the region has effectively embarked on bilateral agreements as building blocks toward an East Asian Community? ASEAN appears to have become more inclined to develop bilateral initiatives. A region-wide initiative does not seem to be the preferred option. Perhaps there are concerns in ASEAN that in a region-wide arrangement it would be overwhelmed by the much larger Northeast Asian region. The combined GDP of the three Northeast Asian countries is currently about 13 times larger than ASEAN's GDP. At the ASEAN Economic Ministers Meeting in September 2002, Singapore Trade and Industry Minister, George Yeo, stated that "[i]t has long been a position of ASEAN that we deal separately with China, with Japan, with Korea in order to secure a certain position for ourselves". (*The Sunday Times* 15 September 2002). It is not immediately clear what this statement exactly means, but the preference for bilateral initiatives is unmistakable.

Indeed, ASEAN's strategy seems to have been reinforced by the favourable response from a number of its economic partners. All of a sudden ASEAN has been brought to the limelight (again). ASEAN will definitely exploit this opportunity in order to be able to come out from the back stage, where it has been pushed to since the financial crisis. It has been reported, Singapore's Prime Minister Goh Chok Tong is now talking about "[t]he ASEAN jumbo jet [that] has one wing in the making in the East, through agreements with China and Japan. India's proposal provides the second wing. With this, we can take off" (*The Strait Times* 6 November 2002). In fact, an ASEAN–US initiative will be much more significant for ASEAN. Singapore officials have also speculated that Korea, which has not offered to enter an FTA with ASEAN, may get into the act next year (*The Straits Times* 6 November 2002). This may be the case. At the APT Economic Ministers Meeting in September 2002 in Brunei Darussalam, it was reported that South Korean Trade Minister Hwang Doo-yun stated that his country was doing a study on the pros and cons of entering into such an agreement with ASEAN (*The Sunday Times* 15 September 2002). Lee Yock Suan, a minister in the office of the Singapore Prime Minister, believes that "[s]lowly but surely, we are seeing the emergence of an East Asian community" (*International Herald Tribune* 4 November 2002).

In addition to going bilateral, it appears that there has emerged an ASEAN understanding that any economic co-operation arrangement today, be it bilateral, sub-regional or inter-regional, should not have a narrow agenda. Any FTA initiative today will have to be of a "new age" type. It can be given any label, FTA, CEP (Closer Economic Partnership) or EPA (Economic Partnership Arrangement), but whatever it is called it is going to have a broad, comprehensive agenda that covers a host of non-border measures in addition to border liberalization efforts.

3.1 ASEAN's Role

As ASEAN has come to the centrestage, and as it emerges as a hub, the big question is whether ASEAN can effectively manage the process. Prime Minister Goh of Singapore rightly asked the question of whether ASEAN can sustain the interests of its partners (*The Straits Times* 6 November 2002). It is clear that ASEAN has to put its home in order first. It has to formulate a comprehensive and coherent AFTA Plus as the basis for developing external, bilateral, and inter-regional linkages. He has proposed to accelerate ASEAN's economic integration toward an ASEAN Economic Community (AEC) as a common market, along the lines of the European Economic Community, by 2020. This, it is argued, is simply a "logical extension of AFTA".

There is as yet insufficient confidence in the region itself that ASEAN can effectively take up this new agenda. Comments refer to the fact that ASEAN "remains so fragmented that any meaningful package within the region seems elusive" (*The Jakarta Post* 6 November 2002). The outgoing ASEAN Secretary General, Severino, in his report to the ASEAN Summit called for political commitment within ASEAN to achieve economic integration. He suggested that ASEAN "seems to have become stuck in framework agreements, work programmes and master plans", and it needs to translate them into concrete actions.

ASEAN must have a strategy for creating both an ASEAN Economic Community and the East Asian Community. They have to be pursued in parallel. In essence, it needs to assure that: (a) bilateral initiatives become building blocks towards an East Asian community; and (b) the various bilateral and sub-regional arrangements will strengthen economic reform efforts within the ASEAN economies. This strategy has to be supported by other East Asian countries. In fact, it should be adopted as an East Asian strategy.

Elements (and principles) of such a strategy have been formulated first by a high-level Task Force on an AFTA–CER FTA, which was headed by Cesar Virata. In addition to WTO consistency, the elements include:

(a) *Comprehensiveness*: it must cover trade in all goods, services (covering all modes of supply), investment, technical barriers to trade, and mutual recognition agreements (MRAs);

(b) *Speed*: the pace of liberalization should proceed faster than that of APEC;

(c) *Flexibility*: some elements of the agreement can be achieved earlier than others (early harvest);

(d) *Simplicity*: the rules of origin in relation to the FTA element must be as liberal as possible and should be simplified and standardized;

(e) *Facilitation*: trade and investment facilitation are to be pursued continuously; and

(f) *Capacity building* is an integral part of the arrangement.

Comprehensive coverage is illustrated by the Singapore–Japan New Age Partnership (JSEPA), which was signed in January 2002. It has two main components. The first is *liberalization and facilitation*. This component covers: trade in goods (including elimination of tariffs), rules of origin, MRAs, trade in services, investment, movement of natural persons, intellectual property rights, paperless trading, competition policy, government procurement, and customs procedures. The second is *closer economic partnership*, which includes: Information and Communications Technology (ICT), human resources development, trade and investment promotion, Small and Medium Enterprises (SMEs), tourism, financial services, science and technology, and broadcasting.

The ASEAN–Japan bilateral initiative, as proposed by Prime Minister Koizumi in January 2002, has also led to a Joint Declaration on Comprehensive Economic Partnership, signed at the Sixth APT Summit in November 2002. The declaration proposed the comprehensiveness not only of sectors but also of *countries*, although allowing for the development of bilateral economic partnerships between Japan and individual ASEAN countries. In addition, it stipulated the following guiding principles: reciprocity and mutual benefits, special and differential treatment (and additional flexibility to the new ASEAN members), to begin in areas where implementation is feasible. The declaration stated that the partnership agreement would include "elements of a possible free trade area" that "should be completed as soon as possible within 10 years, taking into account the economic levels and sensitive sectors in each country". A framework agreement is to be endorsed by the leaders in 2003.

It may well be that the ASEAN–Japan Framework Agreement be modelled and expanded on the Framework Agreement on Comprehensive Economic Co-operation between ASEAN and China, signed in Phnom Penh on 4 November 2002. The Agreement consists of 16 Articles. Article 2 lists the measures for comprehensive economic co-operation to establish an ASEAN–China FTA within 10 years. These include:

(a) progressive elimination of tariffs and non-tariff barriers in substantially all trade in goods;

(b) progressive liberalization of trade in services with substantial sectoral coverage;

(c) establishment of an open and competitive investment regime that facilitates and promotes investment within the ASEAN–China FTA;

(d) provision of special and differential treatment and flexibility to the newer ASEAN members;

(e) provision of flexibility in the negotiations to address their sensitive areas in the goods, services and investment sectors with such flexibility to be negotiated and mutually agreed based on the principle of reciprocity and mutual benefits;

(f) establishment of effective trade and investment facilitation measures, including, but not limited to, simplification of customs procedures and development of mutual recognition arrangements;

(g) expansion of economic co-operation in areas as may be mutually agreed upon that will complement the deepening of trade and investment links and formulation of action plans and programmes in order to implement the agreed sectors/areas of co-operation; and

(h)   establishment of appropriate mechanisms for the purposes of effective implementation of the Agreement.

Substantive articles in the Agreement are: Article 3 on Trade in Goods and Article 6 on Early Harvest. Negotiations in the area of goods trade will involve a gradual reduction or elimination of substantially all products. In the *Normal Track*, the listed products will have their respective applied Most Favoured Nation (MFN) tariff rates gradually reduced or eliminated in accordance with specified schedules and rates (to be mutually agreed upon) over a period from 1 January 2005 to 2010 for ASEAN-6 and China, and from 1 January 2005 to 2015 in the case of the newer ASEAN members. With regard to the *Sensitive Track*, the respective MFN tariff rates will be reduced (and eliminated) in accordance with the mutually agreed end rates and end dates or timeframes. The number of products in the Sensitive Track is subject to a maximum ceiling. The negotiations will also cover other detailed rules, e.g., reciprocity; rules of origin; treatment of out-of-quota rates; non-tariff measures; safeguards; subsidies and countervailing measures and anti-dumping measures; as well as facilitation and promotion of effective and adequate protection of Trade-Related Aspects of Intellectual Property Rights (TRIPs).

An Early Harvest programme has been agreed upon. The products covered by this programme include all agricultural products (chapters 01 to 08) at the 8/9 digit level (HS Code), except those in the Exclusion List. Additional, specific products, negotiated bilaterally, have also been included in the programme (a number of ASEAN countries have not concluded their negotiations). Products under this programme are divided into 3 categories for tariff reduction and elimination:

(a)   Category 1: products with MFN tariff rates higher than 15% for China and ASEAN-6, and 30% or higher for the newer ASEAN members.

(b)   Category 2: products with MFN tariff rates between 5% and 15% for China and ASEAN-6, and between 15% and 30% for the newer ASEAN members.

(c)   Category 3: products with MFN tariff rates lower than 5% for China and ASEAN-6, and lower than 15% for the newer ASEAN members.

Table 2.1   China–ASEAN-6 Early Harvest Timeframes

Product category	Not later than 1/1/04	Not later than 1/1/05	Share in total 1/1/06
	Percent		
1	10	5	0
2	5	0	0
3	0	0	0

For the newer ASEAN members the timeframe is stretched out to 1 January 2010. Vietnam will begin the process before 1 January 2004, while Laos, Myanmar and Cambodia before 1 January 2006. Cambodia's elimination of tariffs will be slower than that of Laos and Myanmar (by one year).

Many observers have expected that the Early Harvest programme will be more substantial than finally agreed upon. The programme covers about 10% of all tariff lines, involving 600 products that belong to the following categories: live animals, meat and edible meat offal, fish, dairy produce, other animal products, live trees, edible vegetables, edible fruits and nuts. Trade between ASEAN and China in products covered by the programme amounted only to about US$860,000 in 2001.

The fact that the Early Harvest programme was not a major "bang" suggests how difficult the follow-up negotiations will be. Future negotiations will be conducted by the ASEAN–China Trade Negotiation Committee (ASEAN–China TNC). One wonders whether the Committee has the ability to deal with the total package covered by the Framework Agreement so as not to get bogged down in the FTA negotiations and yet still be able to produce a significant outcome. This is why the broad-based, comprehensive agreement is so critical to the success of the undertaking. The institutional arrangement must match this task. This is an important challenge for ASEAN as this is ASEAN's first undertaking as a group.

3.2 Developments in East Asia

In East Asia there is a surge of initiatives to form bilateral and sub-regional free trade arrangements (FTAs). The list of such initiatives is rather impressive. However, in the four years since the first initiative was launched with the proposal for a Japan–Korea FTA, only a few have been actually concluded amongst East Asian countries, namely the Japan–Singapore Economic Partnership Agreement (JSEPA) and the ASEAN–China Comprehensive Economic Co-operation Framework Agreement. Some East Asian economies have also concluded trans-Pacific agreements, involving APEC economies. The US–Singapore FTA and the Korea–Chile FTA are the first two. Many others are likely to follow.

Since concluding its first framework agreement with China, which has a FTA component, ASEAN has been courted by other trading partners. A framework agreement is being negotiated with Japan, and will be concluded before the end of 2003. India has made a similar proposal. The US, through Bush's EAI (Enterprise for the ASEAN Initiative), proposed bilateral FTAs with selected ASEAN countries. Having been drawn into the game of bilateral FTAs, the challenge to ASEAN as a group is to consolidate the various initiatives that it and its members are engaged in so as to be able to promote region-wide and global trade liberalization. In the East Asian context today, ASEAN has a specific role that it can play and can carve out for itself in promoting the development of an East Asian Economic Community through trade co-operation and liberalization. In doing so it is not so much a matter of becoming a hub or the hub in East Asia, but more so to prevent it and its individual members from becoming spokes to other hubs that could endanger its cohesion.

The proliferation of FTAs in East Asia needs to be assessed in the context of ASEAN's strife toward deeper integration in Southeast Asia and the desire in East Asia to build an East Asian Economic Community as well as East Asia's interest in a successful outcome of the WTO Doha Development Round.

Bilateral and sub-regional FTAs are being promoted on the assumption that they will produce a kind of "competitive liberalization" as economies are being challenged to undertake more ambitious market opening measures. It is also proposed that the separate agreements can become "building blocks" toward regional and ultimately global free and open trade.

What has developed thus far in East Asia is a sense of "competitive confusion" as it becomes more and more apparent that East Asian countries do not have a clear idea about the dynamics of the processes, specifically the risk of trade fragmentation and political tensions resulting from unco-ordinated processes. The fact that more and more countries are contemplating to join in the FTA game for defensive reasons signals a clear and present danger. Even with the few agreements that have been concluded, it has become more and more apparent that linking them is a rather complicated matter. Although they might not become stumbling blocks to region-wide or global free trade, but they do not necessarily become building blocks either. Rather they may end up being simply "bumbling blocks".

FTAs in East Asia are essentially politically driven. However, politics alone cannot bring about a successfully negotiated outcome. The Japan–Korea FTA proposal was meant to cement a political relationship that greatly improved in the late 1990s. However, it did not come off the ground because the economic benefits from the FTA were perceived to be too asymmetrical to the Koreans. The Japanese side of the joint study, undertaken by IDE/JETRO, showed that if tariffs are eliminated Japan's exports to Korea will expand much more than Korea's exports to Japan, and consequently Japan's trade surplus with Korea will grow by about 35%. In addition, the Korean side of the joint study, undertaken by KIEP, showed a negative income and welfare effect for Korea. In the public symposia on the Japan–Korea FTA proposal held in Seoul and Tokyo, the proposed FTA was strongly opposed by Korean journalists and some business circles as being too premature. Some argued that China should be included to mitigate Japan's economic influence (Kagami 2003).

The Japan–Singapore agreement (JSEPA), signed in January 2002, can be regarded as politically driven as well. In the context of the Southeast Asia's post-crisis development, Singapore sees the need to differentiate itself from the rest and to remain in the radar screen of its major trading partners by going into bilateral FTAs. Negotiations with New Zealand were to provide a training ground. Japan was next, as Japan was looking for a partner with which it can conclude an agreement. Singapore has virtually no agricultural sector and provided a suitable training ground for Japan. One main purpose for Japan to do so is to gradually erode the domestic resistance to agricultural liberalization through a series of FTA commitments. JSEPA has been advertised as a "new age" partnership agreement, some kind of "state-of-the-art" agreement that goes beyond the WTO agenda. Singapore wants to see both its FTAs with New Zealand and Japan (and the more recent ones with Australia and the US) as a way to push others to do the same, and in so doing advances the liberalization at the regional (AFTA, APEC) and global (WTO) level.

It is perhaps still too early to assess the impact of JSEPA that entered into force on 30 November 2002. A preliminary assessment by Leow (2003), described the following benefits of JSEPA. First, tariff savings, which according to the Singapore Ministry of Trade and Industry (MTI), would amount to S$60m per year immediately and S$330m per year within five years. This is presently the main quantifiable benefit. The business community in Singapore, according to Leow, is still unclear about the rules of origin (ROO) that are applied. Second, the agreement provides legal guarantee of services and investment rules. Both Singapore and Japan are legally bound to their services and investment commitments. For instance, Japan has committed to allow up to 1/3 foreign capital participation in Nippon Telegraph and Telephone (NTT). However, it is still unclear whether MNCs operating from Singapore will qualify in Japan. Overall, the commitments in services and investment made in the agreement bind existing *status quo*. No commitments were made to further liberalize existing regimes and many sectors remain unbound. Third, the agreement on investment protection rules provides for an investor-state dispute resolution mechanisms to protect Japanese and Singaporean investors. However, this may not be significant as Japan and Singapore are generally seen as stable investment environments. Fourth, the agreement also promotes economic co-operation on various functional levels between Singapore and Japanese government agencies. However, they are not legally binding. Fifth, the agreement provides "signals to market", namely as a signal for Japanese and Singaporean businesses to move into each other's markets. It cannot be determined whether this is already happening. The Japanese side has made known that the benefit of JSEPA to Japan thus far is the sudden increase of beer exports to Singapore, growing by about 35% since last year. It is also too premature to assess the benefits of the recently concluded Singapore–Australia Free Trade Agreement (SAFTA) and the US–Singapore Free Trade Agreement, which will become effective from 1 January 2004. An interesting provision in the FTA is the *Integrated Sourcing Initiative* that applies to components produced in non-sensitive, globalized sectors, particularly IT and certain medical devices, on which both countries do not impose tariffs. These components, including about 100 IT products, will be treated as being of Singapore origin when they are used in the manufacture of final products in Singapore. For example, qualifying IT components manufactured in Southeast Asia and exported to the US in products assembled in Singapore would be considered to be of Singapore origin.

Singapore has been in the forefront amongst ASEAN economies in the FTA game. The direct effects of its bilateral FTAs may not be significant for the other ASEAN countries. The above examination of Singapore's FTAs also shows that the nature of its FTAs does not lend itself readily to an adoption by other ASEAN countries. However, this should not mean that other ASEAN members should be indifferent to Singapore's undertakings. Singapore may be given the role (by ASEAN) as the first mover, to use the FTA to strategically engage major economic partners in the Southeast Asian region as a whole. Singapore is more readily to do so than other ASEAN countries. However, being given such as role implies that Singapore should fully consult and brief other ASEAN countries on the process and progress of its FTA negotiations. This has not been the practice in the past.

A more consolidated, co-ordinated process in and by ASEAN, including in the development of a common external policy, should be seen as an important element of an ASEAN Economic Community, which is already firmly placed in the ASEAN agenda. While it may give Singapore the role of first mover, ASEAN should have a firm strategy to be involved in FTAs as a group.

For East Asia as a group, Kim (2003) has proposed three possible ways to form a FTA at the region-wide level. The first, most ideal one is to immediately negotiate a region-wide EAFTA. This may prove to be too premature. However, the groundwork can be prepared. The second way involves forming a trilateral FTA in Northeast Asia (China, Japan, Korea) and subsequently link it to AFTA. Its feasibility is being questioned because of difficulties to bring in China into this trilateral undertaking. However, it should be noted that it was China that first proposed to study the possibility of this trilateral FTA (Tsugami 2003). It will be a more difficult proposition if Chinese Taipei (Taiwan) is to be included, which some would consider as only logical (Hakateyama 2003). The third is through various bilateral FTAs between ASEAN and Northeast Asia, and then consolidate them into a pan-regional FTA. This may prove to be a very complicated task unless individual agreements are being designed toward convergence. This suggests the importance of developing guiding principles for the region, which could be applied globally as well.

The initiative by China to negotiate a FTA with ASEAN, which was politically attractive to ASEAN, could be the deciding factor in ASEAN's decision to go into such bilateral agreements. China is the first country that concluded a framework agreement with ASEAN as a group. This could provide a strong incentive for ASEAN to act as a group in developing similar agreements with Japan and Korea or other countries. If ASEAN can become a strong hub and introduce some consistency in its various bilateral agreements, it can turn them into a comprehensive, region-wide agreement. This will make the bilateral initiatives redundant. It is one way to make the building block approach operational.

It is puzzling and also rather disturbing that several ASEAN countries have embarked on bilateral FTA negotiations with the same country that ASEAN has concluded or will conclude an agreement. Thailand is negotiating a bilateral FTA with China. This will be a big blow to ASEAN as it will further reduce ASEAN's ability to play a major role in facilitating the building of an East Asian Economic Community. More important, it threatens ASEAN cohesion and credibility.

Japan too, with its two-pronged approach of negotiating an ASEAN–Japan framework agreement and negotiating bilateral FTAs with selective ASEAN members, is threatening ASEAN's cohesion and credibility (Aquino 2003; Feridhanusetyawan 2003). India too is proposing a FTA with ASEAN but is also willing to embark on negotiating a bilateral agreement with Singapore. Only the EU has consistently insisted to deal with ASEAN as a group at the advice of European companies that are not interested in a fragmented ASEAN market. Thus, a possibly serious fragmentation is currently being observed in East Asia. This fragmentation tends to weaken ASEAN. In turn this will weaken the APT process and thus bring us farther away from realizing the East Asian community idea. Perhaps, efforts to promote region-wide financial co-operation schemes in East Asia could help overcome the regional fragmentation. While Japan has been constraint in playing a constructive role in the trade area, it has great potential to lead in the area of financial co-operation.

4. Financial Co-operation and Integration

East Asia may become an interesting laboratory to test whether monetary and financial, rather than trade and investment, co-operation can become the main drivers for regional economic integration. The prevailing wisdom, inspired mainly by the European experience, suggests a sequencing with trade co-operation far preceding monetary and financial co-operation. As surveyed by Rana (2002), the argument for focusing on trade co-operation is that the benefits from monetary and financial co-operation increase with the level of trade integration. The counter argument is that joining a monetary union could have significant multiplier effects on trade. This argument is supported by a study that shows that trade between countries that share a common currency is on average more than three times what would be predicted from a gravity model of trade.

Proponents of monetary and financial co-operation argue that this kind of co-operation does not require potentially de-stabilizing socio-political measures that accompany more traditional forms of regionalism. They also suggest that monetary and financial co-operation provide participating members more opportunities for "win-win" situations, since it does not involve loss of competitiveness vis-à-vis trading partners and trade diversion as could co-operation in trade and investment (Rana 2002).

Higgot (2000) enthusiastically argued that a "new monetary regionalism" is emerging in East Asia, which may well become "the first region that builds a grouping based on monetary and financial co-operation rather than increased inter-regional trade concentration". The origins of the new monetary regionalism in East Asia can be found in the debate on the creation of an Asian Monetary Fund (AMF) in late 1997 and the agreement between the ten ASEAN countries and China, Japan and Korea to adopt the so-called Chiang Mai Initiative (CMI) in May 2000. These two initiatives, one aborted and the other taking off, were both a response to the Asian financial crisis. Monetary regionalism aims at enhancing the region's ability to weather financial crises. This could be seen as the region's response to the challenges of globalization.

Before the financial crisis, economic integration was essentially market-led. As a response to the crisis, are we seeing the gathering of a momentum for a policy-led integration? (Wang 2002). The crisis was definitely a major catalyst in East Asia's search for an institutional identity. As observed by Stubbs (2002), the crisis has added to the sense of common history that has emerged in the region: "… nearly every government in East Asia felt its reverberations and had to deal with the fallout of the crisis". It also demonstrated the ineffectiveness of APEC and ASEAN as neither was in a position to help the crisis-hit countries. Furthermore, there was resentment with the way the International Monetary Fund (IMF), in conjunction with the US government, handled the crisis by imposing a set of solutions that only served to exacerbate the situation.

Countries in East Asia thus looked to the emerging ASEAN Plus Three (APT) process as the best vehicle for developing a strategy for dealing with future crises. In May 2000, on the sidelines of the annual meeting of the Asian Development Bank (ADB) in Chiang Mai, the Finance Ministers of the APT agreed to pool their hard currency resources. The hope is that this Chiang Mai Initiative (CMI) will become the cornerstone of East Asian co-operation. Can the region build on the CMI to promote further financial co-operation and integration? In turn, can monetary and financial co-operation become the driver for regional economic integration?

Ito (1999) has not come to a conclusion whether monetary and financial integration can precede trade integration. His hunch is that it may not. More important, he is also not convinced that the APT is the right grouping. At present, region-wide processes in East Asia are undertaken mostly under the APT framework. The APT is all what the region has.

The East Asia Vision Group (EAVG) Report did not single out financial co-operation as a core activity toward the establishment of an East Asian Community. It is one of the six areas of co-operation that the Vision Group has recommended. In total, it recommended 57 concrete measures encompassing the six areas of co-operation. The East Asia Study Group (EASG) recommended 26 "implementable" concrete measures, composed of 17 measures for possible immediate implementation and 9 measures for possible implementation in the medium-term or long-term.

In the area of financial co-operation, the EAVG proposed that East Asian governments adopt a staged, two-track approach toward greater financial integration: one track for establishing a self-help financing arrangement and the other for co-ordinating a suitable exchange rate mechanism among countries in the region. Key recommendations by the Group included the following:

(a) Establishment of a self-help regional facility for financial co-operation;

(b) Adoption of a better exchange rate co-ordination mechanism consistent with both financial stability and economic development; and

(c) Strengthening of the regional monitoring and surveillance process within East Asia to supplement IMF global surveillance and Article IV consultation measures.

Recommendations by the EASG may become official policy. Financial co-operation is placed amongst the medium-term and long-term measures. The Group selected two measures, namely to undertake further study (with high priority) on (a) the establishment of a regional financing facility; and (b) the pursuance of a more closely co-ordinated regional exchange rate mechanism.

The EASG left out the Vision Group's recommendation to strengthen the regional surveillance and monitoring process perhaps because such a process is already in place as manifested in the APT Economic Review and Policy Dialogue Process. Indeed, the past few years have seen a number of initiatives to promote financial co-operation and integration in East Asia by groups such as ASEAN, the APT, and ASEM (Asia Europe Meeting).

In his survey, Rana (2002) identified the two main areas of financial co-operation in East Asia, namely: (a) information exchange and surveillance processes; and (b) resource provision mechanisms. The former is seen as a weaker form of co-operation, allowing individual countries to make policy choices in a more informal environment. The latter is in contrast a stronger form of co-operation, ranging from the negotiation of bilateral swaps to the creation of a permanent common reserve pool administered by a secretariat.

4.1 Surveillance

The first regional surveillance process was established in November 1997, the Manila Framework Group (MFG). Higgot (2000) saw this as a significant exercise in the recognition of the "East Asianness" of the region. The Agreement to "Enhance Asian Regional Co-operation to Promote Financial Stability" was "very much part of the wider exercise of soul searching that took place both within ASEAN and between ASEAN and its other East Asian partners". The Group, consisting of deputies from the finance ministries and central banks of 14 Asia Pacific countries, meets twice a year. The ADB, IMF and World Bank provide surveillance reports to these meetings. In addition to surveillance, the Framework included other initiatives: (a) economic and technical co-operation in the financial area ("financial ecotech"); (b) measures to strengthen the IMF's capacity to respond to financial crises; and (c) development of co-operative financing arrangements to supplement the resources of the IMF and other international financial institutions. In its meeting in December 2001, the MFG discussed the proposal by a working group (led by Australia) to establish a "regional financing facility" under this Group.

The MFG is seen by some observers as the pre-eminent forum for regional surveillance and peer pressure. Wang (2002) is of the view that the MFG has not been very successful as a mechanism for regional financial co-operation. First, the MFG has not yet clearly specified the objectives of information exchange and surveillance. Second, there is no actual peer review process in the MFG. Third, issues related to financial sector reform are only discussed cursorily.

In its response to the crisis, ASEAN held a special meeting of finance ministers in Kuala Lumpur in December 1997. The ministers did not come up with any ASEAN financing agreement to assist crisis-affected members. They agreed to renew the ASEAN Swap Arrangement that was due to lapse in August 1999, but did not appear to have examined the reasons why this arrangement had not been used during the early stages of the crisis. Another meeting of ASEAN finance ministers was held in Jakarta in February 1998. The most concrete step taken was to agree on the establishment of a regional surveillance mechanism within ASEAN. It was only in October 1998, eight months after it was agreed on, when the ASEAN finance ministers signed a Terms of Understanding that established the ASEAN Surveillance Process. In fact, the agreement to develop a surveillance mechanism was watered down to a surveillance process. This process is based on the principles of peer review and mutual interest. ASEAN finance ministers meet twice a year for policy co-ordination under this process. The ADB provided the surveillance report, but the reports as well as the results of the meeting are kept confidential. The effectiveness of the surveillance process has been questioned.

Under the APT process, a peer review meeting, the Economic Review and Policy Dialogue Process, was first held in May 2000 in the sidelines of the ADB annual meeting. This process is similar to the ASEAN Surveillance Process. Finance Ministers of the 13 countries also meet twice a year for policy co-ordination. A template to monitor short-term capital flows has been finalized and implemented by several countries under a Japan–ASEAN technical assistance. In May 2001, a study group was established to enhance the process. It recommended a two-phase approach: the first phase is to strengthen the existing process by organizing an additional informal meeting of the APT deputies, and in the second phase an independent surveillance unit is to be established.

The latest development is the establishment of an APT Early Warning System (EWS). This was agreed upon at the APT Finance Ministers Meeting in Honolulu in May 2001. An EWS is being developed with the assistance of the ADB.

4.2 Regional Financing Facility

The idea of a regional financing facility was first proposed by Japan. The financial crisis provided an occasion for Japan to play an important role in the creation of new mechanisms in East Asia through a mix of policies, including financial assistance (Kikuchi 2002). It was Japan that proposed to ASEAN to hold an ASEAN–Japan summit to commemorate the thirtieth anniversary of ASEAN in 1997. ASEAN responded with a proposal to invite the leaders of China and Korea, and this became the first APT (informal) summit. When the crisis hit Thailand, Japan attempted to respond with emergency assistance through the existing framework centring on the IMF. Thailand's liquidity shortfall was estimated at

US$14 billion. The IMF and Japan provided US$4 billion each, but through additional bilateral support, the total package reached US$17.2 billion. These additional funds came from multilateral institutions (such as the ADB) and countries in Asia (including Australia). This showed that the countries in Asia could work together to deal with this kind of crisis. This recognition led to the stepping up of moves within the Japanese government to build a mechanism for a regional financing facility.

The idea of a regional mechanism to stabilize Asian currencies began to launch in Japan in the autumn of 1996, before the crisis struck. This arose from the 1994 Mexican crisis. The view in the Japanese Ministry of Finance (MOF) was that if a similar crisis would occur in Asia, the US and the IMF might not respond as swiftly as they did in the Mexican case. With their combined foreign reserves, countries in Asia could respond to such a crisis if a mechanism exists. A tentative proposal was drafted but before it could be discussed with other countries in the region, the Thai crisis struck (Kikuchi 2002).

It was at the ASEM Finance Ministers Meeting in September 1997 that Japan's concept of an Asian Monetary Fund (AMF) was first discussed. It was also informally discussed at the joint annual meeting of the IMF and the World Bank in Hong Kong in that same month. The idea of an AMF, which would have a nucleus of US$10 billion in capital from the Japanese government, was immediately supported by the Finance Ministers of Indonesia, Malaysia and Thailand. Opposition to this idea came from the United States, China, and the IMF. As a result, Japan was unwilling to pursue the idea further. Instead, the Manila Framework, adopted by a subset of APEC economies in November 1997, was seen as a substitute for the setting up of a regional monetary institution.

As the crisis unfolded, the Japanese government provided large amounts of funds to the crisis-affected countries, mainly through bilateral arrangements. By November 1998, the amount of this funding reached US$44 billion. As its regional approach failed to materialize, Japan stepped up on its bilateral co-operation through the New Miyazawa Initiative that was launched in October 1998. The main elements of this Initiative are as follows: (a) US$15 billion in short-term support for Asian countries; (b) US$15 billion in funds to meet their medium- to long-term financial needs; (c) provision of credits by the Exim Bank of Japan; (d) purchase by the Exim Bank of Japan of bonds issued by Asian governments; and (e) provision of concessional Yen loans by the Japanese government. As part of this Initiative, Japan entered into currency swap arrangements with Malaysia and Korea, which guaranteed the provision of foreign currency reserves in the case of a crisis but without any linkage to IMF conditionality. The second phase of this New Miyazawa Initiative was announced in May 1999. One of its elements is the active use of private sector funds. Another element is to build a regional fund-raising system.

Proposals for a regional monetary fund did not die down. They were raised not only from within East Asia, but also by Europeans and even from the US (Rana 2002).

The desire to develop mechanisms for resource provision within the region led to the adoption of the Chiang Mai Initiative (CMI) by the APT Finance Ministers in May 2000. In addition to reiterating the need for strengthened policy dialogues and regional co-operation activities, the CMI called for:

(a) An expanded ASEAN Swap Arrangements (ASA) that would include all ASEAN countries and a network of bilateral swap and repurchase agreement (BSA) facilities among ASEAN countries, China, Japan and Korea;

(b) Use of the APT framework to promote the exchange of consistent and timely data and information on capital flows;

(c) Establishment of a regional financing arrangement to supplement existing international facilities; and

(d) Establishment of an appropriate mechanism (the EWS) that could enhance the ability to provide sufficient and timely financial stability in the East Asian region.

The ASEAN Swap Arrangement (ASA) was expanded in November 2000 to cover all ASEAN members and the total amount was increased from US$200 million to US$1 billion. The contribution of ASEAN-6 (Brunei, Indonesia, Malaysia, Philippines, Singapore and Thailand) amounted to US$150 million each. That of the rest varies: Vietnam US$60 million, Myanmar US$20 million, Cambodia US$15 million, and Laos US$5 million. The maximum drawdown amount by each participating member is limited to twice their committed amount under the ASA. The swap transactions have a maturity not exceeding 6 months, subject to rollover for a period not exceeding 6 months.

The network of Bilateral Swaps and Repurchase Agreements (BSA) is designed to provide short-term liquidity assistance in the form of swaps of US dollars with the domestic currencies of a participating country. Participating countries can draw on the BSA for a period of 90 days. The first drawing may be renewed seven times. The interest rate applicable to the drawing is the LIBOR plus a premium of 150 basis points for the first and the first renewal drawings. Thereafter, the premium is increased by an additional 50 points for every two renewals, but not exceeding 300 basis points.

The disbursement of funds under the BSA is tied to IMF conditionality. However, it allows for automatic disbursement of up to 10% of the maximum amount of the drawing without any linkage to an IMF programme or conditionality. This limit will be increased as the region develops its own surveillance capacity. The BSA will be reviewed in 2003 (or 2004), with Malaysia's objection to the IMF conditionality as one of the issues likely to be on the agenda. APT members may also decide to make it permanent or even to multilateralize it.

As of end of February 2003, 12 BSAs have been concluded with a total amount of US$31.5 billion. A few others are still under negotiations (See Table 2.2). Japan has been playing a leading role in terms of both number and amount. As stated in the EASG Report, the CMI is seen as a significant step as it is the first concrete agreement among ASEAN countries, China, Japan, and Korea to strengthen co-operation in the financial area. The CMI is also seen as a launch pad from which to broaden and deepen their co-operation and co-ordination to ensure financial stability.

East Asia has definitely moved ahead rather significantly in terms of monetary and financial co-operation. The APT has established semi-annual peer review meetings of finance ministers, efforts to establish an EWS are under way, and through the CMI East Asian countries have began to develop mechanisms to share resources among one another.

Under the APT framework, the region has developed two of the three pillars of regional financial co-operation, namely mutual surveillance and liquidity assistance. The one pillar it has not developed is exchange

Table 2.2   Progress on the Chiang Mai Initiative as of end February 2003

BSA	Currencies	Conclusion Date	Amount
Japan–Korea	USD/Won	July 4, 2001	US$7b (*)
Japan–Thailand	USD/Baht	July 30, 2001	US$3b
Japan–Philippines	USD/Peso	August 7, 2001	US$3b
Japan–Malaysia	USD/Ringgit	October 5, 2001	US$3.5b (*)
Japan–China	Yen/Renminbi	March 28, 2002	US$3b equivalent
Japan–Singapore	--------------------	under negotiation	-------------------------
Japan–Indonesia	USD/Rp	February 17, 2003	US$3b
China–Thailand	USD/Baht	December 6, 2001	US$2b
China–Korea	Won/Renminbi	June 24, 2002	US$2b
China–Malaysia	USD/Ringgit	October 9, 2002	US$1.5b
China–Philippines	--------------------	under negotiation	-------------------------
China–Indonesia	--------------------	under negotiation	-------------------------
Korea–Thailand	USD/Baht	June 25, 2002	US$1b
Korea–Malaysia	USD/Ringgit	July 26, 2002	US$1b
Korea–Philippines	USD/Peso	August 9, 2002	US$1b
Korea–Indonesia	--------------------	under negotiation	-------------------------

Note: (*) The US dollar amount include the amounts committed under the New Miyazawa Initiative, US$5 billion for Korea and US$2.5 billion for Malaysia.

rate co-ordination. Both the EAVG and the EASG have recommended that the region pursue a more closely co-ordinated regional exchange rate mechanism. This item has been put on East Asia's agenda.

Despite great progress, the region has not as yet established the network of institutions to evolve into what Bergsten (2000) had suggested: an East Asian economic bloc. As clearly described by Wang (2002), regional financial institutions range along a spectrum from simple information exchange and informal consultation forums to a supranational entity like the EMU. At the early stage of no institutional integration, governments take note of the policies of other governments without making any attempt to influence them. In view of potential policy spillovers, it may still be useful for governments to exchange information and consult with each other.

ASEAN has moved beyond this stage when they agreed to institute surveillance based on a peer review process, to monitor "developments in ASEAN member countries and in the international economy that could affect individual ASEAN economies and the region". For ASEAN this was the first instance in which ASEAN members will make comments on internal developments. This was seen as a first step in ASEAN's transformation as a regional organization (Soesastro 1998). However, the ASEAN Surveillance Process has been poorly implemented thus far.

In the next stage, when mutual liquidity provision is introduced, it is imperative that monitoring and surveillance mechanisms are in place to control the moral hazard involved. This is the reason why the CMI relies on the IMF and may develop its own independent surveillance mechanism. The final stage, involving exchange rate co-ordination, would require monetary policy co-ordination. Wang (2002) also noted that in the absence of exchange rate co-ordination, incentives for mutual surveillance will be limited because a member country facing a speculative attack may be free to float its exchange rate vis-à-vis those of other neighbouring countries. Under the current APT framework, the purpose of the CMI and mutual surveillance is mainly to prevent the occurrence of financial crises and contagion in the region.

How will and can the region move ahead? Wang (2002) believes that the APT framework is the appropriate grouping for regional financial co-operation because this group has begun to develop a common vision for East Asia. The annual APT summits provide a basis for strong political support. In addition, through the ASEM framework, in January 2001 the finance ministers have launched the so-called Kobe Research Project. The project is designed to facilitate inter-regional research co-operation on issues of monetary and financial co-operation in East Asia, taking into account the lessons learned from the European integration experience.

Strengthening the surveillance mechanism is a key task for further financial co-operation and integration. As reviewed before, the next major task for the APT Finance Ministers is to develop an early warning system (EWS). As argued by Wang (2002), it may be difficult to construct a credible EWS given the lack of reliable statistics in most developing countries. An EWS consists of leading indicators that signal in advance the onset of a crisis. However, not all crises are alike, and thus a "one size fits all" system will not be useful. The MFG and the APT Surveillance Process need to be strengthened. In the MFG, which is based on information provided by the IMF, the World Bank and the ADB, no new or region-specific analysis is presented beyond what is readily available. The process is also felt to be dominated by the US and the IMF. Similarly, discussions in the APT Surveillance Process do not focus on issues of concern and emerging problems.

Malaysia's opposition to linking the CMI to the IMF has led to the establishment of a Study Group to examine how the CMI can develop an independent monitoring and surveillance mechanism. The first meeting of the APT Study Group proposed a two-phased action agenda. The first phase enhances the existing APT process of economic reviews and policy dialogues. The second phase constructs a new strengthened policy dialogue mechanism. The second meeting of the APT Study Group, held in Myanmar in April 2002, failed to reach an agreement on the surveillance issues, except for institutionalizing the APT meetings of deputies for informal policy reviews and dialogues. There is not likely to be an effective surveillance mechanism soon.

5. Conclusion

Current world trade situation is perhaps to a large degree characterized by the many trade policy initiatives that are being pursued at the global, regional and bilateral levels at the same time. Many governments have adopted such policy of moving on *multiple fronts*. This is best exemplified by the US strategy of *competitive liberalization*, in which global, regional and bilateral trade negotiations are seen as complementing and reinforcing each other. With the passage of the Trade Promotion Act 2002, which gives the US Administration fast track authority, it is in the position to pursue what USTR Representative Robert Zoellick called "free trade on the offensive". On the global front, the US has proposed a bold initiative to push multilateral negotiations on the Doha Development Agenda (DDA). This initiative includes significant removal of agricultural subsidies, substantial reduction of agricultural tariffs, zero tariffs on consumer and industrial goods by 2015, zero-for-zero sectoral liberalization as well as liberalization of key services sectors. On the regional front, it is pursuing the FTAA (Free Trade Area of the Americas). It has launched the EAI (Enterprise for ASEAN Initiative) and a similar initiative for the Middle East. On the bilateral front, it has recently signed a FTA (free trade agreement) with Singapore, the first with an Asian country, and has concluded one with Chile. It has begun negotiations with Australia and is also engaged with Morocco, CAFTA (Central American Free Trade Area) and SACU (Southern African Customs Union) in bilateral negotiations. The US, as argued by Feinberg (2003), is not the leader in the global rush toward bilateral and regional free trade agreements, rather it is only playing "catch-up" with the rest of the world. It should be noted that in the late 1980s a similar policy of moving on multiple fronts was also developed by USTR Representative William Brock, producing the US–Israel FTA and a US–ASEAN Initiative (UAI) that never took off.

As suggested by Bergsten (2002), the US remains "the pivotal operator" in the global trading arena. Through its regional and bilateral trade deals the US intends to put pressure on non-members of individual trade agreements either to join the group itself or to conclude a broader agreement. The objective is to accelerate liberalization in ever-widening circles until global free trade is achieved. Its "free trade on the offensive" policy is also, if not mainly, directed toward the European Union (EU). EU's actions will also be decisive in determining the outcome of global trade negotiations. It is the view of the US that Europe badly needs outside pressure to implement internal reforms, especially in agriculture, and that such outside pressure can come primarily from the US.

It should be noted that the use of bilateral FTAs as an instrument to promote global free trade can have political implications due to the selectivity in which such instrument can be used. The EAI as well as Japan's bilateral FTAs with ASEAN will practically be limited to a subset of ASEAN members. The newer members of ASEAN are likely to be left out because they simply cannot take part in the exercise. This can have serious repercussions for ASEAN's cohesion. Both ASEAN and Japan need to re-assess their strategies in taking initiatives in this area.

The issue of leadership is a critical one in the region. As shown before, Japan has provided a *de facto* leadership in the implementation of the CMI as the key provider of financial resources. If the CMI is to become the launch pad for further co-operation, the number and amounts of the BSAs need to be increased. Japan is the only party that has agreed to increase the amounts of the bilateral swaps in order to make the CMI a more credible financing scheme. However, Japan needs to be given greater assurances that their short-term lending will be repaid. As a minimum condition for expansion of the BSAs, Japan wants to see the development of an effective surveillance mechanism in which it can exercise its influence to commensurate with its financial contribution. Japan and China have not been able to agree on a number of operational issues, including the surveillance mechanism. China may not want to grant leadership to Japan in any regional initiative in East Asia. This may be the most serious roadblock to the further development of the CMI

(Wang 2002) as well as to the APT process in general (Stubbs 2002). There is also this strong underlying competition between China and Japan in developing bilateral trade arrangements with ASEAN. The region's preoccupation with the large number of FTAs definitely diverts attention away from the efforts to promote monetary and financial co-operation and integration. More important, however, they may also divert governments from the task of developing the APT process and the building of an East Asian community. ASEAN must take a clear stance on this. It should firmly promote region-wide initiatives and develop relations with all three Northeast Asian countries in a balanced manner. It needs to realize, however, that ASEAN and Japan have already developed deep economic and political relations that are mutually beneficial. This should not be weakened by new initiatives that are misguided.

References

Aquino, Thomas G. 2003. "ASEAN–Japan Comprehensive Economic Partnership". Paper presented at the International Symposium on "FTA: JSEPA and Beyond", organized by the Japan Economic Foundation (JEF) and the Singapore Institute of International Affairs (SIIA), [further referred to as the JEF/SIIA International Symposium], Singapore, 7–8 March.

Bergsten, C. Fred. 2000. "Towards a Tripartite World". *The Economist*, 15 July, 20–22.

———. 2002. "A Competitive Approach to Free Trade". *Financial Times*, 5 December.

East Asia Study Group. 2002. *Final Report of the East Asia Study Group*. Report submitted to the ASEAN Plus Three Summit in Phnom Penh, Cambodia, 4 November 2002.

East Asia Vision Group. 2001. *Towards an East Asian Community–Region of Peace, Prosperity and Progress*. Report submitted to the ASEAN Plus Three Summit in Brunei Darussalam, 31 October 2001.

Feinberg, Richard E. 2003. "The Political Economy of United States' Free Trade Arrangements". Draft of paper presented at the Trade Forum on "Regional Trade Agreements in Comparative Perspective" jointly organized by the Pacific Economic Co-operation Council (PECC) and the Latin American/Caribbean and Asia/Pacific Economics and Business Association (LAEBA), Washington DC., 23 April.

Feridhanusetyawan, Tubagus. 2003. "ASEAN–Japan Comprehensive Economic Partnership: An Indonesian Perspective". Paper submitted to the Institute of Developing Economies (IDE/JETRO), 31 March.

Hakateyama, Noburo. 2003. "EAFTA, Not a Dream but a Reality". Paper prepared for the JEF/SIIA International Symposium, Singapore, 7–8 March.

Higgot, Richard. 2000. "ASEM and the Evolving Global Order". In *The Seoul 2000 Summit: The Way Ahead for the Asia–Europe Partnership,* edited by Chong-wha Lee. Seoul: Korea Institute for International Economic Policy, 11–47.

Ito, Takatoshi. 1999. "Regional Co-operation in Asia: Theoretical Framework, Recent Movements and Prospects". Presentation at the Convention of the East Asian Economic Association, Singapore.

Jayasuriya, Kanishka. 2000. "Asia-Pacific regionalism in the form of 'minilateralism'". *The Strait Times,* Singapore, 18 November.

Kagami, Mitsuhiro. 2003. "ASEAN–Japan Comprehensive Economic Partnerships and Japan's FTA with Other Countries including Korea and Mexico". Comments submitted at the JEF/SIIA International Symposium, Singapore, 7–8 March.

Kikuchi, Tsutomu. 2002. "East Asian Regionalism: A Look at the 'ASEAN plus Three' Framework". *Japan Review of International Affairs.* Spring, 1–23.

Kim, Chulsu. 2003. "Towards an East Asian Free Trade Agreement". Paper presented at the JEF/SIIA International Symposium, Singapore, 7–8 March.

Leow, Edmund. 2003. "JSEPA and its Regional Implications: A Lawyer's Perspective". Presentation at the JEF/SIIA International Symposium, Singapore, 7–8 March.

Rana, Pradumna B. 2002. "Monetary and Financial Co-operation in East Asia: A Survey". *Panorama.* A publication of the Konrad-Adenauer-Stiftung's "Regional Program for Southeast Asia". Singapore, No.2/2002: 17–34.

Soesastro, Hadi. 1998. "ASEAN during the Crisis". *ASEAN Economic Bulletin.* Vol.15 No.3, December, 373–381.

———. 2001. "Towards an East Asian Regional Trading Arrangement". In *Reinventing ASEAN,* edited by Simon SC Tay, Jesus Estanislao, Hadi Soesastro. Singapore: Institute of Southeast Asian Studies, 226–242.

Stubbs, Richard. 2002. "ASEAN Plus Three: Emerging East Asian Regionalism?". *Asian Survey.* Vol.42 No.3, May/June, 440–455.

Tsugami, Toshiya. 2003. "On ASEAN–China Free Trade Agreement — A Personal View from Japan". Presentation at the JEF/SIIA International Symposium, Singapore, 7–8 March.

Wang, Yungjong. 2002. "Prospects for Financial and Monetary Co-operation in East Asia". *Panorama.* Singapore, No.2/2002: 35–53.

3
The Impact of External Changes and Japan's Role in Industrializing Thailand

Somkiat Tangkitvanich and Deunden Nikomborirak

1. Introduction

The fact that Japan has significantly contributed to the industrialization of Thailand can never be overstated. To begin with, Japan is one of the most important trading partners of Thailand. The value of export from Thailand to Japan in 2002 amounted to $10 billion, or about 14.5% of Thailand's total export. The value of import from Japan to Thailand in the same year amounted to $14.8 billion, or about 23% of Thailand's total import. In terms of investment, foreign direct investment (FDI) inflow from Japan to Thailand amounted to $620 million in 2002, second only to the flow from ASEAN.

In addition to the role of the private sector, the Japanese government also plays an important role in promoting industrialization in Thailand through financial support in the forms of loans and grants as well as technical support. The assistance has contributed to both the hardware and the software sides of the Thai industries. The former includes infrastructure development while the latter includes technology transfer, laws and regulation development and institutional building.

During the economic crisis, the Japanese government and private sectors also contributed in alleviating the impact of the crisis. In particular, the Japanese government had initiated a number of projects that aimed at facilitating the recovery of Thailand and other ASEAN countries, most notably the New Miyazawa Initiative. Japanese multinational companies (MNCs) injected capital into their Thai affiliates in the form of loans or equity to retain the level of employment in these firms. Organizations in the third sectors, e.g., the Japanese Overseas Development Corporation (JODC) and Association of Overseas Technical Scholarship (AOTS), also played important roles in developing human resources in Thailand after the crisis. The assistance and co-operation were highly recognized by the

Thai government and private sectors. Indeed, the economic crisis has further strengthened the Japanese–Thai relations.

In future, Thailand and Japan need to deepen their co-operation in areas of mutual benefit. Examples of such areas include human resource development and SME support. The goal of this chapter is to assess the role of Japan in the process of industrializing Thailand in the past decades and discuss some areas for future co-operation.

2. Japan's Roles in Thailand's Industrialization during 1960s–1990s

In this section, we will first discuss the role of FDI in the industrialization of Thailand in general and the role of FDI from Japan in particular. This reflects our belief that FDI is the most important factor that determines the process of industrialization of Thailand. We will then discuss the other roles of Japan in promoting industrialization of Thailand at the sectoral level and its role in developing the necessary infrastructures.

2.1 FDI and the Industrialization of Thailand

Since 1990s, Thailand has always been one of the preferred FDI destinations in Asia. The country ranked fifth in Asia in terms of net FDI inflow during most of the 1990s. From a historical perspective, FDI was a key factor in Thailand's rapid economic growth before the economic crisis in 1997. As a country with political stability, few ethnic or religious conflicts, relatively cheap and hardworking labour, Thailand stood as an attractive FDI destination in Asia for MNCs, especially the Japanese manufacturers.

The value of net FDI inflow to Thailand has increased twelve fold from $189 million in 1980 to $2.27 billion in 1996 (Figure 3.1). The country experienced an average economic growth rate of nearly 8% for three and a half decades until 1996. Despite the world recession in the mid-1980s, the Thai economy was able to expand at double digit rates during 1988–1990, and by over 8% per year from 1991–1995. These high growth rates were largely driven by a steady supply of inward FDI flows. Even during the post-crisis period, FDI was instrumental in the process of structural reform and economic recovery.

At the sectoral level, it would not be an overstatement to conclude that FDI has been indispensable for the development of many sectors, in particular automobiles, electronics and their supporting industries. As a developing country with low technology capability, Thailand would not have been able to build up these industries without FDI. In fact, the 'Asian Miracle' can be attributed to a combination of a favourable external environment as well as the country's ability to make use of FDI to transform itself from an agricultural economy to an industrial one.

Figure 3.1   Net FDI Inflow to Thailand ($US million)

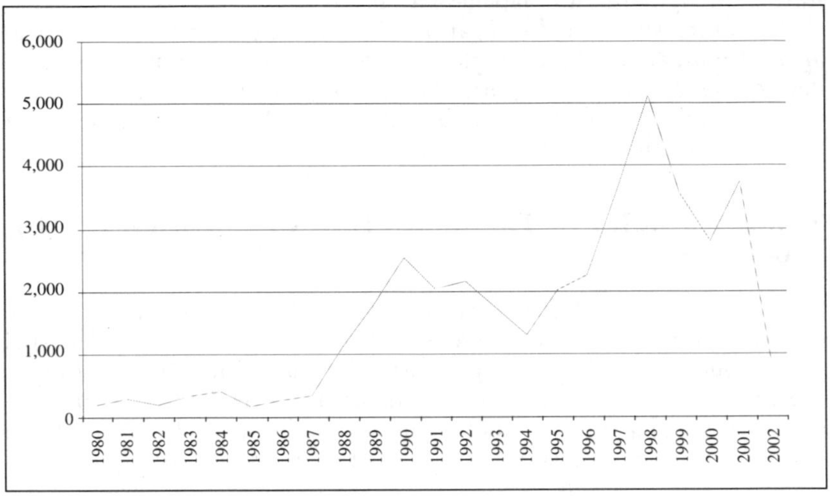

Source: Bank of Thailand.

2.2 FDI from Japan and the Industrialization of Thailand

Sources of FDI in Thailand have been fairly diversified among Japan, the United States, Europe, and Asian Newly Industrializing Economies (Figure 3.2). Japan has been the largest source of FDI in most of the period since late 1970s. Medhi (1997) has categorized FDI flow from Japan into three phases.

The period around 1970s can be described as the period of the first FDI boom, where FDI from Japan increased sharply. The strong Yen and the high labour cost in Japan forced Japanese companies to relocate outside Japan. The first FDI boom was interrupted by the first Oil Shock in 1973. 'Anti-Japanese' sentiments in Southeast Asia, including Thailand, also put a break on FDI inflow from Japan to Thailand. The second half of 1970s experienced another increase in FDI flow from Japan. This represented the second FDI boom. Again the boom was hit by the second Oil Shock at the end of 1970s and the beginning of 1980s. It was not until mid-1980s that investment from Japan was revived, creating the third, and the biggest, FDI boom.

FDI from Japan has accelerated since the Plaza Accord in 1985, which brought about steep appreciation of the Japanese Yen. With the Thai currency pegged to the US dollar, the appreciation of the Yen against the Dollar translated into the appreciation against the Thai Baht. The changing Yen–Dollar exchange rate after the Plaza Accord

Figure 3.2 Net FDI Inflow to Thailand by Sources

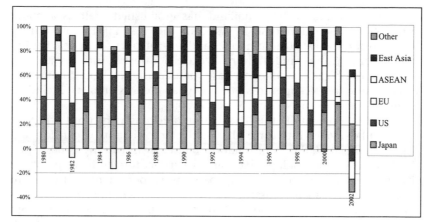

Source: Bank of Thailand.

thus had a significant impact on international trade and investment flow between Japan and Thailand.

A previous study by Kwan (2001), based on regression analysis, noted that each time the Yen appreciated against the Dollar, the economic growth rate of Thailand increased, as was the case between 1986–1988 and between 1991–1995. As such the weaker Yen affects the economic growth in Thailand in a number of ways. One of the important channels was the growth of foreign direct investment. With the cost of production in Japan relative to Thailand increasing, Japanese firms had an incentive to relocate their production bases to Thailand. The net FDI flow from Japan during 1988–1990 constituted about 40–50% of the total net FDI flow to Thailand.

In recent years, however, Japan's share was diluted due to its weak domestic economic conditions. In the last few years Thailand experienced a sharp rise of the FDI from Singapore, driven by its high savings and an outward looking strategy. Most of these investments concentrated in finance, petroleum and real estate in the form of loans to affiliated companies. These contrast sharply with Japanese investments, which focus on share holding in manufacturing companies.

2.3 FDI from Japan and its Role in Sectoral Development

At the sectoral level, FDI from Japan has been indispensable for the formation of many industries in Thailand. This section will describe the role of FDI from Japan in the formation of the automotive and supporting industries in Thailand.

2.3.1 Automobile Industries

With four decades of FDI, Thailand has established itself as a major automobile production base in Asia. In the year 2001, the country produced about 460,000 automobiles and was ranked fifth in Asia behind Japan, Korea, China and Taiwan. Within Southeast Asia, Thailand is currently the biggest production base, particularly for light commercial vehicles (one-ton pickup trucks) for many Japanese assemblers, including Isuzu, Mitsubishi, Toyota and Nissan (Table 3.1).

The development of the Thai automobile industry until the year 2000 can be divided into three phases: cluster formation, expansion and export (Somkiat 2001). The formation phase began in early 1960s when the Thai government adopted a policy to attract foreign investment. By the end of the decade, assembly bases were put in place thanks to investments by Japanese assemblers. The growth of the industry was further stimulated by an import-substitution policy, characterized by high import tariffs and local content requirement. During this period, an initial cluster was formed around Bangkok and Samut Prakarn, a neighbouring province. Domestic sales and production of assembled cars were still low at a level of fewer than 100,000 units per year.

The expansion phase for the Thai automobile industry started in 1980s when the country experienced high economic growth. The rapid growth brought about steep rising trends in the number of automobiles sold in Thailand. The number reached its peak of 590,000 units in 1996. The number almost doubled the sales volume of 300,000 units in 1990. Before the crisis, it was predicted that the Thai domestic market would consume more than 800,000 units by the turn of the millennium. The formation of the ASEAN Free Trade Area (AFTA) also attracted further investment by global assemblers and parts suppliers. Most notably, the U.S. Big Three followed their Japanese counterparts by setting up assembly plants in Thailand, recognizing the country's potential to be the export hub for Southeast Asia. Within a few years, new production capacity was added. Planned capacity exceeded 1 million units in 1999, as shown in Figure 3.3. During this period, the automobile cluster spread to the Eastern Seaboard area where necessary infrastructures were provided by the Thai government.

The expansion phase turned into the export phase when the financial crisis struck Thailand in 1997. The crisis forced several assembling plants to reduce capacity utilization because of the depressed demand. In 1998, the utilization rate dropped to its historical low of 13% and 22% for passenger and commercial cars, respectively. Assemblers were also forced to scale down their investment plans. The transformation of Thailand to an export base was achieved mainly through the decision by Japanese assemblers to sustain a sufficient production level in the country.

Table 3.1 Thailand as a Leader in Automobile Production (production volumes are that of the year 2001)

Assemblers	Vehicle Type	Production in Thailand	World Production	World Share (%)	World Ranking	Asian Ranking	ASEAN Ranking
Mitsubishi	Light commercial	75,743	378,351	20.0	2	2	1
Isuzu	Light commercial	66,228	292,626	22.6	2	2	1
Totyota	Light commercial	45,360	787,794	5.8	3	2	1
Nissan	Light commercial	21,416	568,294	3.8	6	2	1
GM	Passenger	52,059	4,663,399	1.1	12	2	1
Honda	Passenger	42,840	2,608,773	1.6	5	2	1
Toyota	Passenger	34,410	4,424,676	0.8	9	4	2
Mitsubishi	Passenger	8,672	1,242,138	0.7	9	5	3
Nissan	Passenger	3,696	1,966,844	0.2	8	4	1
Ford	Passenger	1,752	3,699,258	0.0	16	2	1
All	Light commercial	298,227	14,228,951	2.1	9	4	1
All	Passenger	156,066	40,144,189	0.4	30	10	3
All	All vehicles	459,418	56,325,267	0.8	16	5	1

Source: International Organization of Motor Vehicle Manufacturers (OICA).

Figure 3.3   Production Capacity of Automobile Industry in Thailand

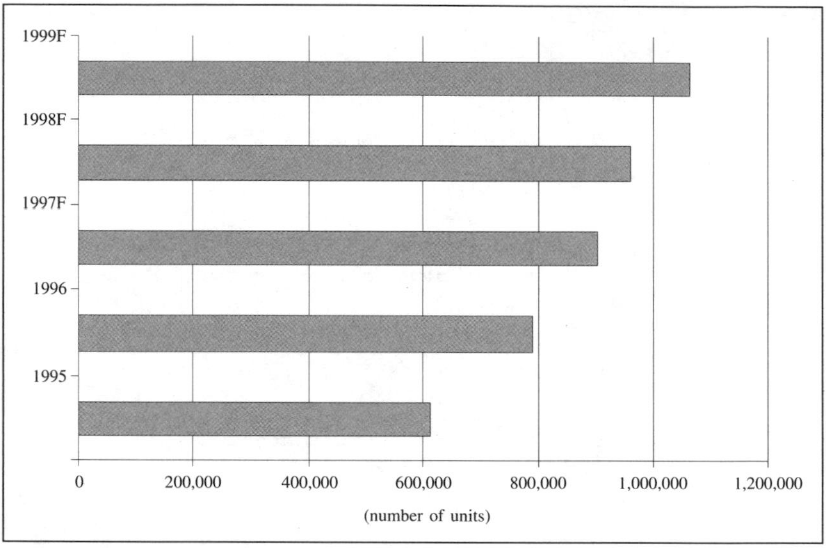

Source: Nipon (2000).

In addition to the private sector, the Japanese third sector such as the JODC and the AOTS also play an important role in the development of the automobile industries in Thailand. In particular, it helps develop necessary human resources through a number of training programmes. The role of such institutes will be discussed in greater detail in Section 3.

2.3.2 Supporting Industries

Supporting industries are broadly defined by The Board of Investment of Thailand as "all industries that supply raw materials, component parts and services required by major manufacturing companies and thereby support these companies' productive activities". While material-process industries such as foundry and stamping industries are typical supporting industries to most industries, the required supporting industries specific to an industry can vary significantly.[1]

The development of supporting industries is important for industrialization in a number of ways. First, strong supporting industries are crucial to successful technology transfers and innovative activities. This is because the development of supporting industries leads to the accumulation of basic technologies. Second, supporting industries contribute to the improvement of trade balance. Without them trade balance tends to deteriorate due to the increase in imports of capital goods required for plant and parts and raw materials required for production. Third, supporting industries promote linkages between domestic industries. Without them, modern industrial sectors and primitive ones would coexist, creating a dualistic structure. Finally, supporting industries tend to support regional development since most of them are based on small- and medium-sized enterprises (SMEs) in labour-intensive sectors.

Supporting industries can be developed in two patterns: the parts-industry traction type and the assembly-industry traction type (Mukoyama 1993). In the former, export-oriented parts industries attract assembly industries, which in turn accelerate their growth. In the latter, supporting industries are induced by backward linkage effects of assembly-industry development. An example of this is the automobile industry in Thailand, where massive investment by Japanese assemblers were followed by that of parts makers. The early waves of FDI from Japan were concentrated on product assembly rather than on parts manufacturing. The development of supporting industries in Thailand by Japanese companies was in part a response to the local content regulation imposed by the Thai government during the period of import substitution.

In addition to the private sectors, the Japanese government also played an important role in developing supporting industries in Thailand. In particular, it assisted the Thai government in establishing the Metal Work and Machinery Industries Development Institute (MIDI) in 1989 to develop metal work and machinery industries. The Institute provides technical advice and services to Thai factories on cutting, grinding, punching, stamping and foundry.

The government, through the Japan International Co-operation Agency (JICA) and other agencies, also initiated a study of the status of supporting industries in Thailand, focusing on the automotive and the electronic industries. The JICA study has identified the strengths, weaknesses and key issues facing assembly industries as well as their supporting industries in Thailand. The study generated much interest among policy makers and significantly raised awareness on the importance of supporting industries.

More recently, the Japanese government, through the Japan External Trade Organization (JETRO) and other agencies, provides technical assistance and a development model for SMEs as a whole. This led to the enactment of the Small- and Medium-Sized Enterprises Act of 2000 and the establishment of the Institute for Small- and Medium-Sized Enterprise Development (ISMED) as the key agency to promote SME development.

However, many problems still remain and successful development of supporting industries in Thailand is still elusive. In particular, the distortion created by high economic growth before the Asian crisis resulted in the shortage of skilled workers, especially engineers and technicians.

As a result, many SMEs in Thailand had difficulties upgrading their technologies and deepening their linkages with MNCs. In addition, as in the case of the automobile industry, once the clusters expanded, there was increasing tension among domestic companies. While additional investment by foreign parts suppliers are welcomed by policy makers and MNCs, it is viewed as a threat by the local industries.[2]

2.4 Japan's Assistance in Infrastructure Development

The Japanese government also contributed to the development of physical infrastructures that are necessary for the industrialization of Thailand through a series of loans, aid and technical co-operation. This section will discuss the development of the Eastern Seaboard Development Program, one of the most successful industrialization programmes in Thailand.

The discovery of natural gas in the Gulf of Thailand in early 1970s gave a strong support to Thailand to begin its industrialization. The development of the eastern region, under the Eastern Seaboard Development Program, was initiated by the Thai government as a part of its fifth National Economic and Social Development Plan. Main components of the Eastern Seaboard Development Plan included the construction of the Map Ta Phut Industrial Estate, which focussed on the development of heavy chemical industries, the construction of the Laemchabang Industrial Estate, which focussed on export-oriented industries, and the establishment of related infrastructures, including ports, roads, and power generation.

Through the Japan International Co-operation Agency (JICA) and the Overseas Economic Co-operation Fund (OECF)[3], Japan had actively provided assistance to the programme. In particular, JICA had contributed to the development of ports and water resources as well as the provision of advice on investment promotion and environment protection.

Due to the programme, industrialization in the eastern region has made significant progress. The region has successfully developed into Thailand's second-largest industrial centre after Bangkok metropolitan area. Investment licensing activities in the eastern regions of Thailand, including the Eastern Seaboard industrial estates, comprised approximately 50% of all licensing activities in the country in 1977, and increased to a total of 64.7% between 1995 and 1997. Of the total 644,000 people newly hired by licensed companies during the same period, approximately 38% of the jobs were generated in the Eastern Seaboard region. Also, per capita income in the Eastern Seaboard region, which reached 2.76 times the national average in 1996, greatly contributed to development in the region (JBIC 2000).

However, many problems still remain. Public utilities and public services remain critical problems for factories in the region. In addition to frequent blackouts/brownouts during the pre-crisis years, many factories complain about costly utility charges and the low quality of services. Finally, red tape and corruption in customs seem to be the chronic problems (Nipon and Somkiat 1999).

3. Japan's Roles during the Asian Crisis

Since the Asian crisis in 1997 to the end of 1998, the Japanese government has announced assistance measures for Asia totalling about $44 billion. The measures include bilateral co-operation in the context of the IMF-led assistance packages, assistance for private investment activities, facilitation of trade financing, assistance to socially vulnerable groups, assistance for economic structural reform and assistance for human resource development.

In October 1998, the Japanese government announced the New Miyazawa Initiative. The Initiative includes a package of support measure of $30 billion, of which $15 billion was to be made available for medium- to long-term financial needs for economic recovery. Another $15 billion was set aside for possible short-term capital needs during the process of implementing the economic reform, known as the Asian Currency Crisis Support Facility.

At the ASEAN + 3 Summit Meeting in December 1998, Japan also announced a scheme of special yen loan facility with the maximum amount of $5 billion over 3 years. The scheme was aimed at assisting infrastructure development, promoting employment and reforming economic structures of Asian countries. Former Prime Minister Obuchi announced a plan for enhancing human resource development and human resource exchanges in East Asia, known as the Obuchi Plan.

In addition to the above assistance and co-operation programmes, the Japanese government, the private sector and the so-called 'third sector' also contributed in Thailand's industrial development and restructuring through a number of programmes. In this section, human resource development in the automobile sector will be highlighted.

As mentioned earlier, the transformation of Thai automobile industry to an exporting industry was achieved mainly through the decision by Japanese assemblers to sustain a sufficient production level in Thailand. The aims appeared to maintain scarce skilled labour in preparation for future demand recovery (Nipon 2001). Since the economic crisis, the JODC and the AOTS contributed to the upgrading of Japanese affiliates in Thailand and other ASEAN countries. This reflected a policy direction from the Japanese government. It has been pointed out that the realization that Japan's manufacturers have already come a long way in completing their Asia-wide production network, which cannot be abandoned because of the crisis (Takahashi 1999).

Between 1979–1999, more than 3,200 JODC experts were sent to developing countries. Among these, about 17% came to Thailand. This makes the country the third largest recipient among developing countries, after Indonesia and China. The programme consisted of two types of services. One was a programme for business development for Japanese affiliates. Under this project, recipient companies were required to pay 25% of the total cost. The rest were subsidized by the JODC. The contents of the training programme included cost reduction, productivity improvement and product development, etc.

The AOTS also provides a training programme for employees of Japanese affiliates in developing countries. The training programme is aimed at maintaining and upgrading the industrial capabilities of these companies. A typical training scheme runs for one week to three months but can be extended to one year if requested by the recipient companies. Under this scheme, the AOTS supports the total cost including personal expenses of the trainees and the cost of training itself and often the cost in bringing experts from Japan. Contents of a typical training programme include production technologies, management techniques, quality control, foreign languages, financial management, cost management, etc. So far there are more than 30,000 trainees from the ASEAN countries participating in the programme, over 10,000 of which are from Thailand.

4. Post-Crisis Reforms in Thailand

After the economic crisis in 1997, the Thai government had little choice but to promote FDI in order to mobilize the much needed foreign capital inflows. Foreign investment liberalization was also an important part of the IMF-led reform package. Planned privatization of state-owned enterprises in infrastructure and de-regulation of key service sectors, such as telecommunications, banking and insurance, were few examples of the post-crisis economic liberalization. In 1999, the Alien Business Law was replaced by the Foreign Business Act, making Thailand's investment regime more open to foreign investors.

The government also amended the Condominium Act in late 1998 to allow unrestricted foreign ownership in condominium or apartment buildings built on land up to two acres. In 2000, the BOI allowed foreigners to own 100% of shares in promoted manufacturing projects. The government also established the Corporate Debt Restructuring Advisory Committee (CDRAC) to monitor and accelerate debt-restructuring process. It also revised the Bankruptcy Act of 1999 and established the Central Bankruptcy Court as a specialized court for bankruptcy cases.

The government realized that simply liberalizing the economy would not be sufficient to boost the competitiveness of the country without restructuring the manufacturing sector. Thus, it issued a number of restructuring programmes and measures. In this section, we will discuss some of the most important initiatives.

4.1 Industrial Restructuring Master Plan

In June 1998, the National Committee for Industrial Development under the former Chuan government issued the 'Industrial Restructuring Plan'. The plan focuses on upgrading Thailand's competitiveness through a set of strategies (Table 3.2). The measures include the allocation of soft loans to the industries in 13 major sectors, the provision of technical assistance through dispatched experts, and the establishment of funds and a number of government organizations to support the industrial development.[4] The budget allocated to the implementation programme amounted to $1.19 billion. A large portion of the fund was financed by loans from the Japanese government under the New Miyazawa Initiative.

Table 3.3 shows the budget breakdown of the restructuring programme. It should be noted that the programme emphasized on upgrading production technology and machinery and relocating labour-intensive industries to the provincial areas. While programmes to improve productivity and upgrade labour skills and product designs were included in the plan, they were only allocated 9.1% of the budget share.

Table 3.2   Industrial Restructuring Plan during the Chuan Government

1. Move toward production of high value-added products for middle to higher markets, with higher quality standards, by
   - upgrading technology and machinery as well as quality management
   - developing product design in line with market preferences

2. Improve efficiency in terms of production costs, streamline production process and improve delivery and quick response as well as improve management capability

3. Upgrading knowledge and production skills of industrial personnel

4. Create strategic alliances to penetrate and expand the markets and to enhance technology transfer

5. Lessen industrial pollution through the adoption of clean technology and industrial zoning policies

6. Disperse industrial employment to regional and rural areas

Source: Ministry of Industry

Table 3.3 Allocation of the Industrial Restructuring Programme Budget ($ millions)

	Loans to Private Sector for:		Allocation to Government Organizations for:			
	Investment	Hiring Experts	Compensation for Experts	Human Resoruce Development	Setting up Organizations	Total
Total Allocation	960.0	27.9	45.2	90.2	68.5	1,919.8
1. Productivity improvement and process restructuring	0.0	19.2	19.2	20.5	5.0	63.9
2. Upgrading production technologies and machinery	375.0	1.8	1.8	2.4	5.0	368.0
3. Upgrading of labour skills	0.0	0.0	14.4	60.2	14.0	88.6
4. Incubating and strengthening small and medium industries	125.0	0.6	0.6	1.4	5.5	133.1
5. Product design and development and distribution channels	0.0	4.8	4.8	5.1	6.0	20.7
6. Relocating labour-intensive Industries to the regions	250.0	0.0	0.0	0.0	33.0	283.0
7. Attracting foreign investment in strategic industries	0.0	0.0	0.2	0.0	0.0	0.2
8. Relocating and containing hazardous industries	210.0	1.5	1.5	0.7	0.0	213.6

Source: Ministry of Industry.

4.2 Tariff Reform

To enhance industrial competitiveness and to conform to international commitments, the Thai government announced a comprehensive reform of the country's tariff structure in late 1999. Under the ASEAN Free Trade Area (AFTA) agreement, import duties would be reduced to 0–5% on 1,190 items on January 1, 2000. Furthermore, under the Information Technology Agreement (ITA), 153 items would be exempted from import duties from January 1, 2000 and another 37 items from January 1, 2005. The reform also focussed on cutting tariffs on capital goods and raw materials. For capital goods, tariffs on machinery, mechanical appliances and parts, electrical machinery, equipment and parts, were reduced. For raw materials, tariffs on input of pharmaceutical, food, chemical, plastic and textile products, were cut. At the same time, the government decided to remove the 10% import duty surcharge on items with a tariff rate over 5%.

The reform directly benefited manufacturers in a wide range of industries. For example, the textile industry gained from lower cotton and chemical tariffs, while the electronics industry gained from lower copper cathode duties. Producers in general would also face lower production costs because of the reduced tariffs on capital goods. At the same time, the removal of the import duty surcharge reduced the degree of protection provided to the industry and encouraged more efficient resource allocation. It was estimated that the government would lose tax revenue of approximately $124 million a year as a result of the tariffs reform. More tariff reform is being planned under the current government led by Prime Minister Thaksin.

4.3 Industrial Diagnosis and Counselling

Since early 2002, the Thaksin government has initiated the Invigorating Thai Business (ITB) programme under the Department of Industrial Promotion, Ministry of Industry. The goal of the programme is to provide technical advice and consulting services to Thai manufacturing companies, focusing on the SMEs. In certain cases, participating companies were required to be diagnosed by industry experts. With the diagnosis counselling services can then be effectively provided to the participating companies. So far more than 2,400 companies have joined the ITB programme.

The diagnosis system was modelled after the Shindan system in Japan. The goal of such system is to analyze the problems in business, production and technology for SMEs and recommend concrete measures to solve the problems. To achieve the goal, a large number of qualified experts (or *Shindan-shi*) need to be trained. The training and certification of experts were conducted by the Technology Promotion Association

(Thailand–Japan), a private, non-profit organization established by the assistance of the Japanese government 30 years ago. Over 200 assistant diagnosers (*Shindan-shi-ho*) have been trained and certified in 2002. An assistant diagnoser is to be qualified as full diagnoser after conducting 10 consultations. The next step is to establish the linkage between the participating companies' access to commercial banks and their diagnosis results.

4.4 SME Support Packages

The Thai government recently announced a series of measures to support SMEs. As mentioned in Section 2, the Japanese government, through JETRO and other agencies, has provided technical assistance and a development model for SMEs. This led to the enactment of the SMEs Act 2000 to promote SME development. The Act, modelled after the Basic SME Act of Japan, also created the SME Promotion Committee whose mandates are to recommend SME Promotion Plan to the cabinet, give incentives and other financial assistance to support SMEs, and direct the Executive Board of ISMED. In addition, the SME Promotion Fund, which provides soft loans to SMEs for business start-ups and upgrading, was set up under the Act.

4.5 OTOP Project

Promotion of micro-enterprises under the Thaksin government has gained a new momentum by the 'One-*Tambon*, One-Product' (OTOP) Project. The project was modelled after the 'One-Village, One-Product' (Isson-Ippin) in Japan.[5] The aim of the project is to promote local industries including SMEs and grassroot industries to strengthen the economy under the concept of 'dual-track' economic policy. Marketing and design are considered key success factors for OTOP products. Japan has co-operated in product design and marketing of traditional handicrafts, e.g., silk, woven baskets, mulberry papers. In particular, since January 2002, it has contributed in collecting prospective products, creating design prototypes, holding an OTOP exhibition in Tokyo, providing guidance for product development and carrying out distribution promotion activities.

5. The Impact of China's Accession to WTO[6]

The accession of China to the WTO is likely to have significant impact on Thailand. On one hand, as China will substantially lower its average tariffs on agricultural products by 2004, Thailand could gain from the increased access to China's big markets after its accession to the WTO. In addition, the Thai consumer will gain from imported cheap Chinese products. On the other hand, as a competitor, China's accession to the WTO will negatively affect Thailand in terms of export and investment attraction.

5.1 Impact on Export

China has developed and expanded its economy rapidly since the opening of the country in 1979. China's accession to WTO will strengthen its product competitiveness in the world market. China is an important trade competitor of Thailand. The two countries produce similar products exported to the world market. Important markets for China exports are Hong Kong, US, Japan, and the EU. Its main import sources are Japan, EU, US and South Korea. According to data from International Trade Center 1999, Thai commodities are more costly compared to those of China. Out of 16 Thai major products, only 6 categories have more market share of the world exports than China. They are rice, fish and shellfish, office equipment and parts, valves and transistor, canned crustaceans, and television. China acquires higher proportion of world market share in another 10 categories including textiles, rubber, jewellery, computer accessories, telecom equipment, radio, furniture, footwear, and electric circuit. The sectors that China have a comparative advantage are textiles, footwear and radio.

Moreover, some of the major markets for Thai exports are similar to those of China. For example, markets for computer and parts (US, Netherlands, Japan); garments (US, Japan, Germany); jewellery and ornaments (US, Belgium); canned seafood (US, Japan); air-conditioners (US, Japan, Spain) and rubber products (US, Japan, and Germany). Comparison between Thai and Chinese exports in three major markets namely, US, Japan and the EU will provide a perspective of international trade relationship between the two countries. For the US import market, the commodity which Thailand is likely to have a comparative advantage over China are frozen shrimps, jewellery, rubber gloves and television. China ranked 5th is coming closer in jewellery export whereas Thailand is ranked 2nd in the same sector (Table 3.4).

Exports from Thailand to Japan that can compete with China's are related to agricultural products such as frozen seafood and chicken. Light manufacturing products have also performed well in the Japanese market. Products that both Thailand and China could obtain a large percentage of market shares include agricultural and labour-intensive products. From Table 3.5, in only four out of thirteen major exports to the Japanese market has Thailand gained a higher market share than China. These commodities include refrigerator, electric circuit, telephone and parts, and frozen shrimps.

Table 3.4   Percentage of Thailand and China Exports to the US

	Thailand			China		
	1998	2000	Rank	1998	2000	Rank
Frozen Shrimps	21	25.27	1	1.42	3.06	10
Jewellery	8.38	12.02	2	2.2	5.92	5
Rubber gloves	21	29.91	2	3.71	6.25	3
TV	6.93	4.49	4	1.19	2.39	5
Electric fan & Air Pump	2.94	3.68	11	15.15	20.57	1
Transformer	3.14	4.11	6	18.57	20.95	2
Radio	1.1	2.44	10	36.21	25.28	2
Computer Accessories	0.93	0.9	15	8.73	13.61	2
Computer and parts	5.55	5.77	8	6.39	10.33	5

Source: Department of Business Economic from Jakkapong (2001).

Table 3.5   Percentage of Thailand and China Exports to Japan

	Thailand			China		
	1998	2000	Rank	1998	2000	Rank
Refrigerator	32.48	34.31	1	6.11	25.95	2
Electric circuit	1.57	1.27	1	1.18	1.48	8
Telephone & parts	4.9	11.62	2	7.97	7.9	3
Frozen shrimp	7.29	8.32	4	3.7	4.05	6
Frozen fish	14.76	15.39	2	10.8	17.81	1
Frozen chicken	25.7	25.59	2	41.4	47.75	1
Processed seafood	36.41	32.92	2	28.28	34.4	1
Computer accessories	1.69	2.34	8	12.02	15.31	3
Computer and parts	7.24	5.16	9	3.98	8.96	4
Air-conditioner	21.69	30.72	2	27.31	41.16	1
TV	17.34	12.42	3	22.23	30.79	2
Furniture	9.76	9.22	3	14.32	26.43	1
Diode/Transistor	13.65	9.47	6	8.44	13.43	2

Source: Department of Business Economic from Jakkapong (2001).

In contrast to the other two markets, exports of agricultural products to the EU were not so successful for both China and Thailand. Products that both Thailand and China could gain a high percentage of market shares are also labour-intensive or light manufacturing products. China was able to penetrate quite completely into the EU market for light manufacturing products such as telephone, transformer, radio, and leather shoes. Thailand, on the other hand, was successful in labour-intensive products such as jewellery. From Table 3.6, jewellery, processed fruits,

Table 3.6 Percentage of Thailand and China Exports to the EU

	Thailand			China		
	1998	2000	Rank	1998	2000	Rank
Jewellery	8.12	10.43	2	2.62	5.65	6
Processed fruits	5.67	6.67	3	1.86	1.75	8
Recorders	12.65	13.48	3	4.15	10	5
Air-conditioner	4.54	9.46	3	2.59	6.07	4
Telephone and parts	1.15	0.65	12	3.44	3.47	4
Transformer	2.12	1.34	11	8.37	11.53	2
Radio	1.82	1.27	18	19.14	20.42	2
Sweater	1.99	3.37	5	4.65	6.32	3
Computer and parts	1.69	1.5	11	2.14	4.81	6
Leather Shoes	1.17	1.02	16	3.84	5.53	3

Source: Department of Business Economic from Jakkapong (2001).

recorders and air-conditioners are the only four products that Thailand has a larger market share than China. However, China is also a significant competitor in exporting those products, specifically Chinese jewellery, which could compete not only in the US, but also in the EU markets.

WTO membership will grant China the equal rights as those of other members including Thailand. This will widen the competitive gap between Thailand and China. It will reduce Thailand's export opportunities of labour-intensive products and light manufacturing commodities to the world market.

5.2 Impact on FDI

More adversely, China's accession to the WTO will attract substantial capital inflow to China due to its sources of comparative advantage and large domestic market opportunities. Not surprising, China has become one of the most popular destinations for foreign direct investment. In 2000, total FDI inflow to China was $6.8 billion of contractual value and $3.5 billion of realized value consisting of 364,345 projects. Hong Kong has the largest share in FDI to China, accounting for 52.7% of total projects and approximately 48% of FDI value followed by US, Japan, Taiwan and Singapore. The FDI is invested mostly in the industrial sector, accounting for 60.9% of total value.

Total FDI inflow into China has exceeded $300 billion, far beyond that of the ASEAN countries since 1993. China's WTO accession will provide another increase in the FDI inflow to China due to its comparative advantage in labour, natural resources and its huge domestic market. The emergence of China as an attractive destination for investment has diverted the flow of foreign direct investment from Southeast Asian countries.

Concerning investment from Japan, China has become the most attractive location for many Japanese MNCs, even before its accession to the WTO. In a survey of planned FDI in the next three years by Japanese manufacturers, China emerged as the leading destination (JBIC 2002). Thailand has always been a distant second or third most popular FDI destination for Japanese MNCs after China and the US. The accession of China to the WTO is thus viewed as a threat to ASEAN's FDI.

A survey by JETRO in late 2001 (JETRO 2002) somewhat soothed the worries of Thailand and other ASEAN countries that although one-fifth of Japanese MNCs planned to relocate production sites from Japan and other countries to China after its accession to WTO, 99% of those with investment in ASEAN countries replied that they would not relocate to China (Figure 3.4). This is because many Japanese companies are still concerned about the investment climate in China, particularly about the rules relating to establishment, the transparency of investment rules, and the tax system.

Realizing that Thailand cannot directly compete with China in terms of market growth, production costs and labour supply, the Thai government is positioning itself as an investment destination for MNCs that would like to diversify the risks of investing in China. In particular, it highlights the attractiveness of the country in terms of better transparency of investment rules and tax system and the stability of the country. The response of Thailand is also to improve its attractiveness by de-regulating industries and restructuring domestic structural

Figure 3.4   Planned Relocation of Production Sites of Japanese MNCs to China

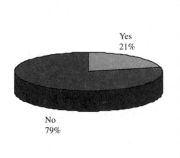

From	Share of 'Yes' (%)
Japan	67.5
Hong Kong	9.0
Taiwan	6.6
Korea	1.2
Malaysia	3.0
Singapore	1.8
Indonesia	1.2
Philippines	1.2
Thailand	0.6
Other Asian Countries	1.2
Mexico	1.2
USA	4.2
United Kingdom	1.2

Source: JETRO (2002).

problems as well as establishing the AFTA by 2002 to enhance production networks across the region. Initiatives taken by these countries to improve their investment environment to maintain foreign investor interest, together with the additional business opportunities following the increase in intra-regional trade and trade-supporting services industries, should create a new impetus for the region's continued economic growth.

6. Reorienting Japan's Policy Towards ASEAN and Thailand

Thailand and Japan should continue to hold policy dialogues and seek to build new co-operative structures so that they can act together under a new partnership to achieve future prosperity in Asia. There are urgent issues that Thailand must address in order to successfully compete in the global market and promote sustainable growth. These are areas where the co-operation between the two countries is likely to be fruitful.

6.1 Human Resources Development

Thailand must continue its educational reforms and endeavour to further spread secondary and higher education. It will also need to place particular emphasis on training engineers and the skilled workers who will support its industries. Japan should provide active support for human resources development in Thailand by promoting academic exchange at the university and graduate school levels and mutual exchange of students and teachers. It should also make use of the Yen loans and send in retired engineers to train engineers in Thailand. In addition, Japan should provide support for public and private programmes in Thailand to train skilled workers. As part of the reform of Japanese education currently in progress, it is necessary to create an environment that makes it comfortable for students from Thailand to study in Japan.

Human resource development assistance should not be limited to schooling or even training in manufacturing industries, but should be extended to cover new areas, e.g., IT and high technology. One step towards the new direction is the collaboration between NECTEC and Japan's Ministry of Economic, Trade and Industry (METI) which have jointly developed a national IT professional examination for Thailand similar to the system which is popular in Japan.[7] Similar initiatives are also conducted in other Asian countries, e.g, India. The Japanese government has announced that it may allow foreign IT professionals that passed the examination to work in Japan. This is certainly welcomed.

6.2 SMEs Promotion

SMEs are at the core of the supporting industries that will enable Thailand to form a competitive industrial structure. We see the need for co-operation between Thailand and Japan not only in areas where the Thai industry is currently strong, but also in new industries such as IT and high technology. In this regard, we look forward to further initiatives by the Thai government to improve the investment environment of the country.

SME promotion is an area in which Japan provides significant contribution. Japan can use Yen loans and the dispatch of experts to provide active support for the strengthening of SME finance, human resources development, and technology and management skill improvement. Japanese companies will also need to be more active in the transfer of technology and in the exchange among engineers so as to build closer and more co-operative relations with Thai companies. The "Small Business Rebuilding and Development Fund" established by the Asian Development Bank (ADB) and others will provide a means of facilitating capital injections to SMEs. These capital injections should, together with the advisory services provided by the fund, help Thailand to build a more competitive industrial structure.

Notes

[1] For example, in the case of the textile industries, supporting industries include textile processing industries (e.g., fibre manufacturing, spinning, dyeing and fabricating) machinery industries and petrochemical industries that produce the raw materials for synthetic fibres. In the case of automobile industries, supporting industries are generally referred to direct and indirect parts suppliers. Direct suppliers are those that supply parts and raw materials to assemblers. Indirect suppliers can be further classified into raw materials and parts suppliers and equipment suppliers. Examples of the first group are suppliers that provide parts made of leather, plastic, rubber, or supplying paints or petrochemical products. The second group operates in the so-called 'supporting industries', supplying moulds and dies, jigs and fixtures or providing forging, casting, tooling, cutting, surface treatment, heat treatment services.

[2] This is exemplified by a proposal of the Thai Auto-Parts Manufacturing Association (TAPMA) to the Ministry of Industry in October 2002 calling for protection of the domestic industries. The proposed protections include limiting investment privileges for foreign investors, reintroducing local content requirements and allocating at least 30% of the government's automobile procurement budget for vehicles with at least 60% of local parts (TAPMA 2002).

[3] The two institutions are merged to be the Japan Bank for International Co-operation (JBIC).

[4] Organizations that have been established include industry-specific institutions, e.g., the Textile Institute of Thailand, the National Food Institute, the Electronic and Electronics Institute, and the Vehicle Institute, and functional institutions such as the National Productivity Centre and Industrial Design Institute. Examples of Funds set up are the Fund for Venture Capital Investment, the Thailand Recovery Fund, etc.

[5] A *tambon* is a local administrative unit consisting of many villages.

[6] This section is drawn from Jakkapong (2001).

[7] Currently only one subject, the Fundamental IT Engineer Examination, is introduced and so far there have been only two examinations since the year 2001.

References

Hidehiko, Mukoyama. 1993. "Development of Supporting Industries in ASEAN: A Case Study of Thailand". Pacific Business and Industries. Vol. IV, 1993.

Jakapong, Uchupalanand. 2001. *China's WTO Accession and its impact on Thailand*, Thailand Development Research Institute.

JBIC. 2000. *Eastern Seaboard Development Plan Impact Evaluation*. Japan Bank for International Co-operation. Available at <www.jbic.go.jp>.

———. 2002. "JBIC FY2001 Survey: the Outlook of Japanese Foreign direct Investment". *Journal of the Research Institute for Development and Finance*, No 9, January, 4–38.

JETRO. 2002. "JETRO Toshi Hakusho 2002". Japan External Trade Organization, Tokyo.

Kwan, C.H. 2001. *Yen Bloc: Toward Economic Integration in Asia*. Washington, D.C.: Brookings.

Medhi, Krongkaew. 1997. "Japanese Direct Investment in Thailand". In *Evaluating the Japanese Participation in the Thai Economy*, Japanese Studies Centre and Thammasat University.

Nipon, Poapongsakorn. 2001. "Skill Formation in the Thai Auto Parts Industry". Manuscript, Thailand Development Research Institute.

Nipon, Poapongsakorn and Somkiat, Tangkitvanich. 1999. "Post Evaluation for Eastern Seaboard Development Program". Submitted to JICA and OECF.

———. 2001. "Industrial Restructuring in Thailand: A Critical Assessment". In Masuyama S., Vandenbrink D. and Yue C. (2001), *Industrial Policies in East Asia: Towards the 21ˢᵗ Century*. Nomura Research Institute and Institute of Southeast Asian Studies.

Somkiat, Tangkitvanich. 2002. "SME Development in Thailand's Automotive Industry". A draft paper submitted to the Institute of Southeast Asian Studies.

Yoshi, Takahashi. 1999. "Technical Assistance to Japanese Affiliates: The Case of Autoparts Industry in Thailand". In *Industrial Linkage and Direct Investment in APEC*, edited by Satoru Okuda. Institute of Developing Economies. Available at <http://www.ide.go.jp>.

Yoshihiro, Otsuji and Kunihiko, Shionoda. 2002. "Building Closer Ties with ASEAN: Industrial Co-operation and Future Direction". Presented at the First Japan–ASEAN Research Institute Meeting. Bangkok, 25 October, 2002.

4
Confronting Regionalism in Asia: A View from the Philippines

Gwendolyn R. Tecson

1. Introduction

The Asian financial crisis can be said to have been the fruit of East Asia's own success as late-comer economies. Led by the NIEs in the late eighties and early nineties, the East Asian firmament was studded by high-flying economies, with the possible exception of the Philippines that caught the attention of the world for having defied the Kuznets 'law' of growth. They grew but without passing through a phase of social inequity. Their stunning growth performance easily became fuel to capital flows that accelerated with every good news. With growth came naturally the self-confidence that made these countries bring down their defenses, albeit prematurely, that previously guarded their markets of both goods and capital. It was generally a period of euphoria where daily trading in world capital markets reached $1.26 trillion in 1995, or seventy times the volume of world trade, considering that the ratio was only 10:1 (at a daily trading of $80 billion) only a decade-and-a-half earlier (Rana and Yap 2001). In such a heady environment, bad news eventually snowballed into a crisis of confidence and quite quickly led into the contagion that made investors run over one other to beat an exit. Between 1996 and 1998, $95.6 billion of private capital flows were reversed for the five crisis-affected countries, or equal to 10% of their GDP.

The Philippines was some kind of an outlier in this miracle story of East Asian growth. Considered the 'basket case' or the 'sick man' of Asia, the eighties were a lost decade for her, still struggling as she was with the political and economic instability that were the aftermath of the Marcos dictatorship. But now by hindsight, it is commonly judged it was precisely its historically weak economic performance relative to its more successful neighbours that made her appear less vulnerable to the international 'hot money flows' that plagued the countries in the region.[1] Moreover, the country's relatively repressed and inefficient financial systems had earlier led to crises in the '70s and '80s, and forced the Philippine government to undertake a number of important financial sector reforms in the'90s (to be discussed in Section 2, following). As a result of these reforms, not only did the quantity of financing, but also its quality had improved, to such an extent that on the eve of the crisis, the Philippine financial system was judged more solid than that of its Asian neighbours (Noland 2000, p. 4). Even the high lending rate policy at the time proved to be beneficial in that property developers adopted more conservative approaches to financing and thus were less over-leveraged than their Thai counterparts (Hutchcroft 1999. Cited by Noland 2000, p. 4). This, together with the central bank's imposed ceilings in June 1997 on banks' loan exposure to the real estate as well as on the permissible collateral valuation of real estate security, helped minimize the banking system's level of non-performing loans from the non-tradable sector. Moreover, the country was able to redirect its domestic lending boom to finance the overcapacity in the tradables sector and thus was able to exploit better the ensuing real peso depreciation through an increase in exports rather than a compression of imports (Noland 2000, p. 4). Nevertheless the Philippines, though relatively less affected than its neighbours, did suffer from slow-down effects of the regional crisis and has not fully recovered from it, given the decline in economic activity that has since become global, and this in spite of the policy reforms undertaken in the financial and the real sector of the economy for over a decade now. We shall now turn to a discussion of these policy reforms in the succeeding section.

2. Policy Reform in the Philippines Before and After the Regional Crisis

As discussed in the previous section, policy reform in the Philippines started long before the regional crisis, making her less – though not completely – vulnerable to the adverse effects of the crisis. These were policy reforms that addressed the costs that necessarily accompanied the benefits of growth of late-comer countries. Hirono (2002) had argued that sooner or later, the late-comer countries of Asia would have to come to terms with the costs of late-comer country growth. That is, they will have to address the policy and institutional distortions and rigidities that had accumulated over time as a consequence of continued high-growth, the benefit of being a late-comer. In spite of much lower growth performance, such distortions and rigidities likewise accumulated in both the real and the financial sectors of the Philippine economy, so policy reform had to address both.

2.1 Reform of the Financial System

The Philippine banking sector was historically 'repressed' or 'partly repressed' , according to a survey of the financial system of 34 countries (Williamson and Mahar 1998), in terms of six dimensions: credit controls, interest rates, entry barriers, bank autonomy, privatization, and international capital flows. The policy of limiting bank branching side-by-side with high capital requirements that encouraged mergers and consolidations effectively gave market power to incumbents, thus discouraging market contestability and competition. Indeed, in terms of net profit to total assets, interest rate margins, average difference between deposit and lending rates, and overheads as a ratio of total assets, Philippine banks often topped the average for seven Asian economies (figures cited in Gochoco-Baustista and Reside 2001, p. 91). The limitations to branch banking weakened the deposit mobilization process (Lamberte and Lim 1987). It was no wonder that the country notoriously had the lowest saving and investment rate in the region: 21% and 18%, respectively, as against the average (1997–2004) of 34% and 24% respectively for ASEAN-5. High profits coupled with high intermediation costs was a tell tale sign of a lack of competition. Moreover, measures of concentration merely confirmed the commonly-held idea of an inefficient banking sector.

With such a financial system that was prone to instabilities and crises, the government then undertook in the early nineties a number of significant reforms. Branch banking was initially allowed in the rural areas in the late eighties (Lamberte and Llanto 1993) but it was only in 1992 that restrictions on new bank entry and branching were relaxed effectively. New domestic banks were also allowed to enter the market, so long as they met the minimum capital and prudential requirements of the Monetary Board. Moreover, geographic restrictions on bank branching were dropped in 1993, allowing banks to open branches anywhere in the country, subject to prudential requirements such as capital adequacy, liquidity, profitability and soundness of management (Paderanga 1996). The result was that the number of branches more than doubled, from 1,957 at the end of 1990 to 3,145 at the end of 1995 (Fritz-Krockrow 1999). Moreover, the moratorium on the entry of foreign banks, upheld ever since the establishment of the Central Bank of the Philippines in 1949, was lifted in 1994, partially liberalizing the entry and scope of operations of foreign banks in the country. Ten new foreign banks were granted licences in 1995, each entitled to six branches, and since then seven locally incorporated foreign bank subsidiaries have been approved. The period was one of overall reform of the system, with the Central Bank being rehabilitated into the new Bangko Sentral ng Pilipinas (BSP) and the consequent strengthening and improvement in the quality of its prudential regulations. The result was to infuse more competition into the system and to encourage financial deepening[2] as well as to contribute to a managerial and technological upgrading of the system, partly driven by a reverse drain of returning Filipino bankers who were employed as expatriates by foreign banks (Noland 2000, p. 3). As previously mentioned, the BSP also imposed ceilings on banks' loan exposure to the real estate sector in June 1997 as well as on the permissible collateral valuation of real estate security. Coupled with a much smaller real estate boom relative to its Thai counterparts, the banks were much less exposed to this sector on the eve of the crisis.

Nonetheless, there were still many pockets of weakness in the country's financial system. With the de-regulation of the foreign exchange market in 1992 came the lifting of restrictions on foreign exchange transactions by banks as well as a re-definition of prudential limits on foreign exchange positions (Gochoco-Bautista and Reside 2000, p. 92). Moreover, the re-entry of the Philippine government into the international capital markets may have resulted in an increase in the foreign indebtedness of the private banking and private non-bank sectors. Thus, with the onset of the financial crisis in 1997, came an increase in NPLs (non-performing loans) in the banking sector, rising from 4.67% in December 1997 to 13.1% in June 1999. By December 2000, it stood at 15.1% of the total outstanding loans of commercial banks, mostly due to private corporate debt.

Once again a flurry of reforms in the sector was undertaken in order to strengthen the system against system risks and improve its regulatory oversight. The General Banking Law of 2000 was passed aligning domestic banking standards with international best practice and improving regulatory oversight. Various regulations were likewise passed by the BSP to improve asset quality and risk management, such as: (1) the adoption of risk-based capital adequacy standards aligned with international norms; (2) strengthening of transparency with respect to NPLs, classified loans and other risk assets, and DOSRI loans (to directors, officers, stockholders, and related interests); (3) the requirement for banks wanting to provide electronic banking services to set up the necessary risk management practices; (4) the shift of focus of supervision from a purely compliance-based and checklist-driven assessment to a forward-looking and risk-based framework. Moreover, the BSP adopted an early intervention system and a bank resolution strategy allowing it to deal more effectively with problem banks and thus to safeguard the soundness of the banking system. It also undertook special programmes to modernize and strengthen government banks through privatization and adopted measures to reduce the intermediation costs of financial institutions (Gochoco-Bautista and Reside 2000, pp. 96–97). The BSP has also begun to supervise banks on a consolidated basis to include their foreign currency exposures (NEDA: Medium-Term Development Plan of the Philippines or MTPDI, 2000–2004, p. 3).

In view of the abuses committed in the securities market, the Securities Regulation Code (SRC) was passed in July 2000 to strengthen the regulatory framework over the securities market. Of course, this does not preclude more positive reforms that must address the weakness of the capital market. The market itself remains underdeveloped due to such imperfections as the lack of private bonds for long-term financing of the corporate sector as well as the presence of obstacles to its development, such as the taxation on secondary instruments e.g., the documentary stamp tax (DST). It is believed that the activation of a secondary market for loans will increase the economy's resilience to banking crises (Gochoco-Bautista and Reside 2000, p. 113). An active secondary market will facilitate risk-pooling and risk-spreading. It will provide benchmarks for the market-based valuation of financial assets like loans and other types of securities.

On the other hand, the NPLs of the banking system are no more than reflections of the financial distress of firms and corporations. For instance, of the top twenty firms that filed for debt relief with the Securities and Exchange Commission (SEC), eleven filed for suspension of payments at the start of the Asian crisis. Of the 103 companies seeking debt relief in 1997, manufacturing made up about 34% and construction/realty firms about 20% of total (Securities and Exchange Commission or SEC, cited by Gochoco-Bautista and Reside 2000, p. 101). In this regard, reform must be adopted to strengthen the firms' legal and regulatory infrastructure. For this a number of reforms must be made at the level of the Securities and Exchange Commission, the government institution in charge of corporate supervision. For instance, the SEC must improve corporate disclosure and transparency rules, adopt formal rules for implementing corporate rehabilitation, and make proceedings swift and time-bound, and creditor-, rather than regulator-driven (Gochoco-Bautista and Reside 2000, p. 112). Already reform in the SEC is underway, specifically the policies to strengthen financial discipline in the corporate sector and strengthen the legal framework for protection of creditors' rights, subject to Philippine laws and jurisprudence (BSP: Supplementary Memorandum on Economic and Financial Policies, 30 June 1999). It is envisaged that over the medium term, the quasi-judicial function of the SEC will be transferred to the court system under a new bankruptcy law.

2.2 Trade and Investment Policy Reform

Past industrialization policy in most of the developing-country world had been of the import-substituting type. It is a matter of fact that the economies that had realized the inimical effects of such a policy on efficiency and growth earlier were precisely those that grew fastest. These were the NIEs that had either liberalized their trade sector completely (e.g., Singapore) or those that effectively mitigated the impact of their import-substituting strategies on their economic incentive and export structure (e.g., South Korea). The Philippines, realizing the futility of such a protectionist strategy whose policies had been by and large held captive by vested interests, finally embarked on a unilateral tariff reform and import-liberalization policy in the early eighties, designed culminate in 2004 with a uniform tariff policy of 5% on all goods. The average (nominal) tariff rate had therefore been gradually adjusted downward from a high 28% in 1985 to about 8% in 2000 in a series of phases of tariff reform that started in 1981. Moreover, as a result of the Import Liberalization Programme, the number of regulated items of the total tariff lines went down from 34% in 1985 to 3% in 1996 (De Dios 1997).

At first glance this policy reform might be construed as a rash measure that will open the production sector to the global winds that could only wreck it. But the indicators show that such a policy reform carried over a period of two-and-half decades actually made for a more efficient, fast growing albeit leaner production sector and unleashed the export-potentials of the economy (Tecson 2000). Indeed for the first time after over two decades of trade deficits, the trade balance turned positive in 1999 and 2000. While this was partly due to a rapid decline in imports due to the economic slowdown after the financial crisis, the other half of the story is that exports managed to grow in spite of all odds.

Hand in hand with trade liberalization came liberalization in the foreign direct investment sector. In 1991, the Foreign Investment Act was passed, allowing foreign equity participation of up to 100% in all areas, except those left in the negative list, which was subsequently shortened through legislation in 1996. Restrictions are thus only limited to investments in two areas: those which are reserved for Filipino nations by virtue of the Constitution or specific legislation, such as mass media, co-operatives or small-scale mining (Negative List A) and those areas included in the list (Negative List B) by virtue of defence, risk to health and moral, as well as protection of small-and-medium industries. Rights of foreign investors are guaranteed by the Constitution, such as remittance of earnings, freedom from ex-propriation and requisition of investment, and full and immediate repatriation of capital and remittance of dividends without prior approval by the BSP so long as these have duly been registered with the Bank.

Generous incentives have also been made available to investor-locators in the country's economic zones. A recent World Bank comparison of government incentives provided by other export-processing zones in the region suggests that the country's package of benefits and other incentives is not only competitive but can be easily considered "the most generous and flexible set of incentives available anywhere". Duty-free import privileges are said to be without parallel in its provision of full exceptions in perpetuity for export and free trade enterprises for almost all project-related inputs, whereas other countries either restrict such privilege to production-related items or those not available locally, or is made available only once. Moreover, the range of promoted activities in the country's ecozones is very broad, allowing services, utilities, infrastructure development, and tourism accommodations in addition to manufacturing.

However, in the context of the present economic slowdown, protectionism is rearing its ugly head. There is a current clamour for a postponement of the 2004 deadline for the decline in manufacturing sector tariffs to a uniform 5% for all commodities. With the government's decision to ask for an AFTA waiver to exclude its petrochemical industry from the 2003 deadline (to allow it to keep its 15% tariff) the trade agency (Department of Trade and Industry or DTI) has been deluged with requests for similar privileges. In particular, full-page ads have been taken out by the downstream plastics industry to protest the privilege given to the petrochemical industry, while their own products will be included in the 5% uniform tariff policy. 2004 being a presidential election year and given the weakness of the economic sector, one can expect the protectionist tendencies to prevail.

2.3 Reform in the Services Sector

In addition to the reforms in the banking sector discussed earlier, a number of landmark reforms have been adopted in important areas of transportation and communications. De-regulation of the **telecommunication industry** began in 1993, with the issuance of Executive Order (EO) 59 which compelled the inter-connection of all telecommunication facilities, thus de-monopolizing the industry long-held by the Philippine Long Distance Telephone Co. (PLDT) since pre-war days. As a result, new players entered the industry and firms expanded their networks, while introducing new technologies and services. Technological change also caught up with the industry with the introduction of cellular phone systems. Riding on such changes, the government required in 1993 the installation of mobiline telephone systems and international gateway facility operators of 400,000 and 3M telephone lines, respectively within five years.

Likewise, in the **maritime industry** long-awaited reforms came with the liberalization of rules governing the entry of new operators for existing routes, the de-regulation of the entry of newly-acquired vessels into routes already served by franchised operators and allowing the re-routing of existing vessels. Moreover, de-regulation of domestic shipping rates and acceleration of the de-monopolization and privatization of public ports nationwide were undertaken. These reforms resulted in greater competition in the industry, leading to the provision of better and greater variety of services at cheaper rates, as well as modernization of facilities and capital infusion by incumbents (Austria 2001).

Liberalization and de-regulation of the **domestic air transport industry** came about with policy reform in 1995 with the elimination of restrictions on domestic routes and frequencies, as well as on government controls on airfares and charges. Such reform definitely infused greater competition into the domestic air transport industry leading to lower airfare as well as improvement in the quality of service. However, reform in the international air transport industry, while allowing in principle at least two official carriers for the country, stopped short of true liberalization, with the industry dominated by the Philippine Air Lines (PAL), currently owned in the majority by an influential private individual.

In the **energy sector**, private sector initiatives were harnessed through build-operate-transfer (BOT) schemes in the provision of electricity through private investments in power-generating projects (including by foreign operators) as well as through the passage of the Omnibus Power Industry Bill in 2001 which paved the way toward privatization in the industry.

Also in 1997, the **downstream petroleum industry** was de-regulated allowing more suppliers and market-driven pricing of petroleum products. In the same year, privatization of the **water system** came with the sale of the Metropolitan Waterworks and Sewerage System (MWSS) to two private consortia of local and foreign investors.

3. Regional Environment in Evolution

While a number of reforms have taken place in the Philippines, the regional landscape has not stood still. A number of changes had taken place that are of importance to the Philippines. In the following subsections, we shall discuss such changes and their implications on the Philippines, both present and future.

3.1 Entry of CMLV and its Implications on ASEAN

The four new ASEAN members, namely Cambodia, Laos PDR, Myanmar and Vietnam, are economies emerging from centrally-planned systems. As such, they have a number of adjustments to make in order to join the league of market-economies of the older six member-economies of ASEAN. Relative to the latter, all available statistics show that the newest four member-economies are at the bottom. Fig. 4.1 indicates that they have the lowest per capita incomes among the ASEAN members, indicating the degree of catching up they are expected to accomplish. Myanmar's per capita income is only 0.13, Cambodia 0.24, Laos PDR 0.29 and Vietnam 0.41 of the ASEAN average per capita income of $1,124 for the year 2000. Consequently, they are importing and exporting the least among the economies of ASEAN, as well as drawing the least in terms of FDI (Fig. 4.2) implying that they are at the moment the least connected with the rest of the world. Three of them – Cambodia, Laos PDR, and Myanmar are not members of the WTO as such their products are unable to take advantage of greater market access to WTO members.

Politically, it is important that they are not left to turn back to other economic alternatives because this could lead to destabilization in the region, if not the world. Hence, there is a strong need to uplift these economies at all levels, politically, socially, and economically. Coming from a battle-scarred past, each of these economies is endowed with people who are basically intelligent and tenacious, but who have lost decades of possibilities at all fronts. Thus, while some ASEAN economies

Figure 4.1 Per Capita Income of ASEAN Countries, 2000 (in US Dollars)

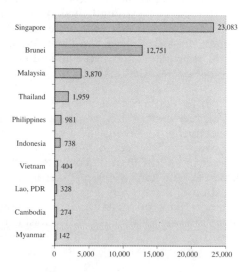

Figure 4.2   Inward FDI in ASEAN, 1990–2000

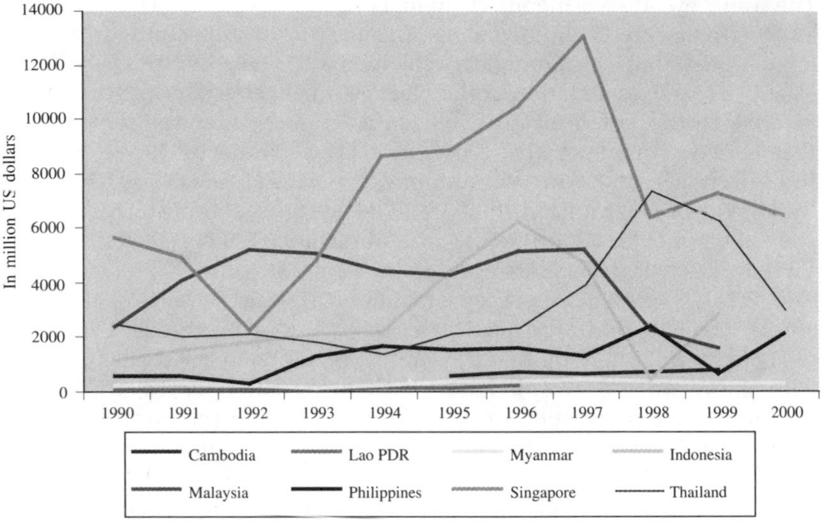

Source: International Financial Statistics 2001: IMF, 2001.

are in the process of doing it alone in making bilateral FTAs with other economies (e.g., Singapore with Japan and New Zealand, and eventually with Australia, there is talk of Thailand and the Philippines, separately, with Japan) and while there are talks of enlarging the regional reach with a possible FTA between AFTA and China, it is important that the internal cohesion of the ASEAN be strengthened. Another reason for the urgent need for the newer members to integrate with the rest of the ASEAN is to eliminate the need for a two-track ASEAN wherein the second tends to ask for 'flexibility' and 'special and differential' treatment in trade and other types of negotiations with the other more advanced group.

Studies by the World Bank have shown that the formation of regional integration arrangements (RIAs) could have different effects on whether economies converge or diverge as a result of the RIA. Their results indicate that countries with comparative advantage closer to the world average do better in an RIA than do countries with more extreme comparative advantage (World Bank 1999, p. 15). The reason for this lies in the possible relocation of industry in response to differences in factor endowments and hence factor prices. Although it is possible that the very unskilled labour-intensive industries will relocate to the capital-scarce new members, the lack of the requisite capital assets (especially transport and telecommunications) may militate against it, leading to divergence rather than convergence in future incomes. This is the reason why the EU has a regional policy that mobilized large resource transfers to the poorer member-economies. It is clear that this policy has paid off, especially in Ireland, which had been a net recipient of such regional transfers.

It is for this reason that in the Hanoi Declaration of 23 July 2001 (see Appendix), the foreign ministers of the different member-economies of the ASEAN asserted the urgent need to address the 'development gap' between ASEAN members. This Declaration recalls the previous commitments of ASEAN regarding this, such as in the ASEAN Vision 2020 at the second informal ASEAN Summit in Kuala Lumpur in 1997, during which the ASEAN members expressed the desire to promote equitable economic development and the reduction of poverty and economic disparities in the ASEAN region, and in the Hanoi Plan of Action adopted at the Sixth ASEAN Summit in Hanoi in 1998; which prescribed concrete measures to reduce the development gap among ASEAN member countries and to promote the economic integration of the new member countries into ASEAN. Then again the ASEAN leaders adopted the Initiative for ASEAN Integration (IAI) at the Fourth Informal Summit in Singapore in 2000, an initiative that gives direction to and sharpens the focus of collective efforts in ASEAN to narrow the development gap within ASEAN as well as between ASEAN and the other parts of the world. The Hanoi Declaration of 2001 calls, among other things[3], for the special efforts and resources to promoting the development of the newer member countries of' ASEAN (Cambodia, Laos, Myanmar and Vietnam or CLMV) with priority given to infrastructure, human resource development, and information and communication technology. (Hanoi Declaration 23 July 2001, p. 1).

In the field of **infrastructure**, activities/projects are lined up with the objective of improving access, efficiency and quality of transport and energy infrastructure networks. Proposed projects under the infrastructure sector of the plan include:

- studies for the Singapore–Kunming Rail Link Project in Cambodia, Laos, Myanmar and Vietnam (CLMV);
- the Integrated Strategic Regional Development Plans for the development of the ASEAN highway network in the CLMV countries; and
- the institutional strengthening and capacity building for CLMV energy sector.

Under **human resource development**, projects are lined on capacity building for the civil service sector; such as, developing policy framework and programmes in the labour and employment sectors, as well improving higher education systems. While in the **information and**

communication technology (ICT) sector, activities are planned primarily to focus on narrowing the digital divide within ASEAN by implementing the e-ASEAN Framework Agreement. Moreover, the CMLV will be drawn into closer integration with regional economy through the building of institutional capacity and human resources in such areas as customs, national standards, quality, metrology and investment (http://www.aseansec.org).

3.2 Closer Economic Partnerships: ASEAN and East Asia

The ASEAN keeps the fire burning in East Asia by holding discussions with its dialogue partners (ASEAN + 3, or Japan, South Korea, and China) right after its annual summits of ASEAN leaders. There are currently serious talks on the formation of closer regional alliances particularly with Japan and China.

3.2.1 ASEAN and Japan

Ever since the United States dropped its initial misgivings about regional integration arrangements and even became proactive by creating the NAFTA in 1993 and currently the Free Trade Area of the Americas (FTAA), the global market has not been the same. Indeed the division of the international market into regional blocs continues unabated. Currently, about 150 of 200 such RTAs are in force, of which about 100 were created since 1995 (WTO website: www.wto.org/regionalism). Japan which has for a long time been out of membership of any RTA has changed her mind. It has recently concluded a FTA with Singapore. And in the most recent Summit at Phnom Penh in 5 November 2002, the leaders of the ASEAN nations and of Japan had accelerated the process of forging regional alliance through the creation of Comprehensive Economic Partnership (CEP). A mandate has been given to develop a framework for the CEP to be presented during the next Summit in October 2003. It is a far-reaching regional agreement that is expected to bring not only economic benefits to the member-countries, but also regional stability. For this reason the CEP has been envisioned by the Expert Group (see *Expert Group Report on the ASEAN–Japan CEP*) to rest on such principles as comprehensiveness, reciprocity, mutual benefits, while taking into consideration the disparities in development levels among ASEAN members.

3.2.2 ASEAN and China

The most recently concluded summit, the eighth, was singular in that the leaders managed to sign a framework of agreement that would commit them to establish a China–ASEAN Free Trade Area within ten years, beginning 2010. This came apparently after Premier Zhu deftly overcame the objections raised initially by Pres. Arroyo of the Philippines, PM Mahathir of Malaysia and PM Goh Chok Tong of Singapore. While the two former leaders raised objections on creating a FTA with China specifically on the need for flexibility in the face of weakness of certain of their countries' sectors relative to China, PM Goh Chok Tong of Singapore is supposed to have raised a more fundamental point, namely, the viability of the ASEAN itself when it forms a FTA with China. He expressed his fear that forming a FTA with China might threaten the internal cohesion of ASEAN, a cohesion that must first be realized by ASEAN as an economic bloc, so that it could negotiate with China as an equal.

Why does ASEAN need to forge an ASEAN–China FTA? Presumably ASEAN harbours fears of the 'dragon' that is emerging in China. Given its drawing power for foreign direct investment flows, China has not only surpassed many times over the ASEAN inward capital flows and may have even competed away such flows that would have been destined to ASEAN. PM Goh therefore expressed all of ASEAN's collective hope when he asserted that ASEAN is an excellent alternative to China for FDI. Forming a FTA with China may possibly lead to a diversion of some capital inflows toward ASEAN, as multinational investors find the need to diversify their investments. Moreover, the huge Chinese market offers lucrative potentials to ASEAN producers, especially in agricultural products. Indeed the current trade surplus of ASEAN vis-à-vis China (about $12 billion in 2002) is one of the points singled out by the Chinese Premier as demonstrating that a FTA with China will be to ASEAN's favour. China has already offered a 'downpayment' in terms of lower tariffs on certain agricultural products from ASEAN in order to sweeten the deal.

Judging from the eagerness of China in forging a FTA with ASEAN in the future, one could raise questions on the reasons for such eagerness. Beyond Premier Zhu's statement that

> we are not seeking a special status in the region, we do not seek to dominate in any way but are motivated *solely by the desire to foster the prosperity of the East Asian region as a whole, especially Southeast Asia* (italics supplied)

> http://www.dfa.gov.ph

one could speculate on the real objectives of China in forming such a FTA. For one, China wants to lessen its dependence on the West by taking advantage of the dynamic market at its Southeast Asian backyard. Moreover, given the pace of RIA formation in the West – that is, with the Free Trade Area of the Americas (FTAA) in the works and the current enlargement of the European Union – China naturally feels that it has to belong to a regional alliance. Indeed, other than APEC which is not a real RIA, the three East Asian countries of Japan, South Korea, and China, do not belong to any RIA. Surely there are other geo-political and economic reasons for wanting to join ASEAN.

3.3 ASEAN and India

Since 1992, India has been a dialogue-partner of ASEAN. In the last ASEAN Summit at Phnom-Penh, on 5 November 2002, the first ever ASEAN–India Summit was held. During the Summit the leaders of each nation committed themselves to jointly contribute to the promotion of peace, stability and development in the Asia–Pacific region and the world, and respond positively to the challenges of a dynamic and regional and international environment.

4. The Challenge of Regionalism

As a member of the ASEAN, the Philippines is now confronted with a totally new environment that promises even greater challenges in the years ahead. By 2010 ASEAN will be entering into free trade area arrangements with China. The CEP deadline with Japan is less certain but there are fall back arrangements. Japan has already concluded a free trade area with Singapore; it has expressed its desire to have one with the Philippines and most probably with Thailand. India is keen on developing a long-term relationship with ASEAN and to co-operate with it in many areas of common interest (see *The Joint Statement of the First ASEAN–India Summit*, 5 November 2002, Phnom Penh, Cambodia, and *India's ASEAN Report* by the Confederation of Indian Industry), although India is for the moment engaged in maintaining its South Asian character in focusing primarily its attention on the SAPTA (SAARC Preferential Trading Area).

The unmistakable trend toward more intensified competition is already written on the wall. The potential of a large domestic market coupled with vast amount of cheap labour resources will continue to attract a big chunk of FDI into the productive sectors of China, thus constituting an edge that no ASEAN country nor even AFTA as a whole can hope to replicate. China is touted by some analysts[4] as a possible candidate to replace Japan in the future as a possible driver in the region due to the latter's seeming inability to emerge from its prolonged recession. And India which has long stagnated economically is emerging with new found strength, armed with comparative strength particularly in IT.

How then does the Philippines prepare for such an environment? The Philippines cannot remain indifferent, because to stand still in such a regional environment means to fall behind the others that are charging ahead.

Following are some key areas that must be addressed if the Philippines is to benefit from the new regional and global environment that she is now facing.

4.1 Continued Liberalization

It is true that the economic slowdown in the country's trading partners has snowballed into the Philippine economy. The poor economic performance of the manufacturing sector, however, has been attributed almost solely to the liberalization policy which has opened the economy to greater trade. On the other hand, the new found strength of the export sector, which until recently has remained anemic when compared to those of other trading neighbours in the region, has never been attributed to the liberalization policy which has reduced much of the import barriers to manufactured materials and components. Because of the trade policy reform, about half of the tariff rates are now at 3% and these are mainly levied on imports of manufactured materials and components. However, since the trade reform policy had not been completed, about 40% or so of tariffs have remained in the 7–20% range, mainly consisting of finished goods. Considerable effective rate of protection is thus accorded to finished manufactured import substitutes, whereas a uniform tariff policy of 5% was envisioned to reduce EPRS to approximately 5% in 2004.

Protectionism has quite unmistakably started to rear its ugly head. Early this year, the Secretary of the Department of Trade and Industry had announced that in line with the 'protectionist stance' of the President, the Philippine government "was likely to keep the duties within their WTO bound rate (or tariff ceiling)" (Philippine Daily Inquirer, 13 January 2003). This would, in effect, put a brake on the government's tariff liberalization programme, since the Secretary has been quoted as saying that the Philippines had been too hasty in cutting down its applied tariff rates way below the bound rates. Moreover, encouraged by the plans of other ASEAN countries to seek exceptions to the AFTA deadline of 2003, the Philippine government has decided to ask for a similar exception for the petrochemical industry, in the name of 'national interest'. The ability of an industry to turn the head of the country's leaders has thus opened the floodgates for other industries to ask for similar exceptions to the liberalization process.

And yet, the regional integration arrangement is about dismantling barriers across national boundaries in the region in order to encourage the flow of goods, factors of production, and services among member countries. The Philippines, after Thailand, has the longest road to travel in achieving the AFTA deadline, given that the proportion of imports with 0% tariff remains at 96% by the year 2003. Unless the country decides to embark on the path of continued liberalization, much of the dynamism that the trade policy reform has injected into the economy will be dissipated.

On the other hand, liberalization is not enough. As argued by Bautista and Tecson (2002) the lack of a stable and sustained income growth in the country during the two decades of trade liberalization is proof of the reality that liberalization is not a 'stand-alone' policy. Without the necessary complementary policies and the right institutions to implement these policies, trade liberalization will simply lead to a shrinkage of the productive sector. As the experience of the recent past has shown, the trade reform efforts had been undermined by real exchange rate appreciation, fiscal imbalance, external debt problems and indeed by overall political and social instability that is enough to stop all growth on its tracks. The trade reform policy, therefore, together with the relevant complementary policies, must be vigorously pursued.

4.2 Relentless Pursuit of Macroeconomic Reforms

Central to growth is the macroeconomic environment in which such growth is embedded. The seeming inability of the Philippines to extricate itself from the ravages of the Asian financial crisis long after its more affected neighbours have gotten back onto the growth trajectory is due to a large extent to fiscal imbalances: poor tax collections vis-à-vis ballooning government expenditures. The result is a serious cutback in government activity side by side with the slowdown of the private sector together with huge debt overhang, both foreign and domestic. Unless the government is able to improve its revenue collection while introducing greater efficiency into its expenditure activity, such fiscal imbalance will not only lead to deeper debt problems but will also de-stabilize the exchange rate, and hence undermine any effort at trade liberalization.

Moreover, greater competition must be injected into the economy and it must come not only from the stimulus of a more open trade regime. For unless the domestic market is geared to greater competition, there will always be a pressure to seek protective cover from the government. Moreover, only healthy competition will be favourable to continuous upgrading (both product and process) and which constantly pushes the entire productive sector to the limits of the efficiency frontier, will make the country move forward, let alone survive, in a such an environment.

4.3 Increased Productivity, the Key to Future Growth

East Asia's success story has been linked to its record of openness to trade, macroeconomic stability and human capital formation. Unfortunately such a spectacular record has eluded the Philippines, until it has decided to bite the bullet with regard to protectionism and macroeconomic stabilization. Its record of human capital formation, though quite high by developing country standards, is fast being whittled away by inefficiency and lack of funding. Only in the '90s was it able to attract the waves of FDI, particularly of Japanese capital, that had helped finance much of the development of its neighbours. However, like its other neighbours, it has to confront the critical problem of how to create linkages between FDI-created growth areas and the rest of the economy. For understandably the dynamic sectors were confined within the economic zones which remain unconnected with the domestic economy but were almost completely turned to foreign sources of raw materials and components and foreign markets for their products. Value-added was limited to the measly contribution of labour and provision of certain peripheral services. Almost non-existent was the chain of suppliers of components and other raw materials that had gradually linked the rest of the economies, say Taiwan or Singapore, with foreign-owned firms in the industrial zones.

Growth in most of the developing countries of Asia, including the NIEs like Singapore, has been led for the most part by foreign multinationals which were in search of an export base. International productions networks have thus emerged, and the developing countries have become part of that technological revolution. Factor accumulation has undoubtedly created some growth in the past, even in the Philippines, but this is no longer enough for the future. The country has already lost its comparative advantage in terms of unskilled labour-intensive production in the face of the vast armies of labour in China and Vietnam, and even South Asia. At the same time, it has not accumulated enough physical capital to make a clear shift of its comparative advantage. Its current fallback is its remaining pool of semi-skilled labour resources, a possible advantage which might be very temporary, given the deterioration in the quality of education in the country and the fast catching-up in educational investments particularly in the sciences and math among our neighbours. Already the heat of competition can be felt and this will intensify with greater integration. The only way to go is to keep ahead of the pack. The real challenge, then, according to a recent World Bank study (*Innovative East Asia: The Future of Growth*, World Bank, January 2003) is how to *enhance productivity through innovation.* According to Mr. Wolfensohn of the World Bank:

> This transition from factor-intensive to productivity-driven growth, and from imitative to innovative growth is undoubtedly going to be bumpy. Implementation will be difficult.... And yet, the opportunities are there. East Asian countries are already starting from a position of strength – with the adequate supply of resources, the manufacturing skills, the educational and research infrastructure, and the base of financial and business services. Most are increasingly open and competitive economies. East Asia is poised for another major step forward. It will be fascinating to see the extent to which the vision is transformed into reality.

Transformation of the vision into reality will not come naturally. It will require investments in both the software and the hardware, that is, in human capital formation and ICT infrastructure. Above all it needs vision, of the kind that is proactive in view of emerging technologies and the competitive pressure of the external environement.

Notes

This chapter was written for the Workshop on "The Implications of External Factors to ASEAN's Development and Japan's Role", sponsored by the Japan Institute of International Affairs, Tokyo, Japan, 19–20 April, 2003.

[1] M. Noland (2000) reports that because the Philippines was underweighted in the Morgan Stanley Capital International (MSCI) Far East Ex–Japan Free Index, the benchmark against which the performance of mutual funds investments in the emerging markets of Asia is usually compared, the country was relatively less exposed to the mutual fund investments because mutual fund managers tended to stick rather closely to the index in their country allocations (p. 5).

[2] The ratio of money and quasi-money to national income was seen to have doubled from 23% to 49% between 1986 and 1996 (Noland 2000, p. 3).

[3] To this end, on August 15–16 2002 at the ASEAN secretariat in Jakarta, Indonesia, a development co-operation forum involving representatives of the ASEAN member economies will be held for ASEAN's dialogue partners as well of international agencies to discuss the details of the regional approach.

[4] This possibility is, of course, a long shot. As Prof. Hirono points out, there are a number of reasons why China is far from replacing Japan as a driver in the region. Among these are: 1) China's sustained economic growth during the last two decades may not continue forever under increasing

contradictions taking place in China in terms of both regional and personal income disparities and serious implications of state-owned enterprise reforms that will have to be accelerated if China has to sustain its economic growth and social stability; 2) China's trade and investment relations with ASEAN are less than one tenth of Japan's trade and one-1000th of Japan's FDI in ASEAN, if one excludes Taiwan's investment in ASEAN; and 3) China will be pressured by the international community to accelerate her domestic economic, social, environmental and political reforms which of course will have serious implications on her sustained economic growth and export expansion.

Appendix
Hanoi Declaration on Narrowing Development Gap for Closer ASEAN Integration

WE, the Foreign Ministers of the ASEAN Member countries representing Brunei Darussalam, the Kingdom of Cambodia, the Republic of Indonesia, the Laos People's Democratic Republic, Malaysia, the Union of Myanmar, the Republic of the Philippines, the Republic of Singapore, the Kingdom of Thailand and the Socialist Republic of Vietnam;

ACKNOWLEDGING that the benefits of globalization are at present unevenly distributed and that the development gap among nations and regions would *be* further widened without effective measures to address the negative impact of globalization;

RECALLING the commitment of the ASEAN leaders, proclaimed in the ASEAN Vision 2020 at the Second informal ASEAN Summit in Kuala Lumpur in 1997, to promote equitable economic development and the reduction of poverty and economic disparities in the ASEAN region and in the Hanoi Plan of Action adopted at the Sixth ASEAN Summit in Hanoi; in 1998 prescribing concrete measures to reduce the development gap among ASEAN Member Countries and to promote the economic integration of the new Member Countries into ASEAN: and

EVOKING the decision of the ASEAN leaders on the Initiative for ASEAN Integration (IAI) adopted at the Fourth Informal Summit in Singapore in 2000, giving direction to and sharpening the focus of collective efforts in ASEAN to narrow the development gap within ASEAN as well as between ASEAN and other parts of the world;

Do hereby declare:

1. We resolve to promote, through concerted effort, effective co-operation and mutual assistance to narrow the development gap among ASEAN Member Countries and between ASEAN and the rest of the world for the sake of dynamic and sustained growth of our region and prosperity of all our peoples.

2. We shall work together to identify, through research, analysis and consultation, the comparative strengths of our economics and their potential for complementary, with a view to promoting regional economic integration and a sense of community and shared responsibility among our nations.

3. We shall devote special efforts and resources to promoting the development of the newer Member Countries of ASEAN (Cambodia, Laos, Myanmar ,and Vietnam or CLMV) with priority given to infrastructure, human resource development, and information and communication technology.

4. We renew our call *for* the development of the region through sub-regional co-operative programmes, including the ASEAN–Mekong Basin Development Co-operation, the Brunei–Indonesia–Malaysia–Philippines East ASEAN Growth Area, the Indonesia–Malaysia–Thailand Growth Triangle, the Indonesia–Malaysia–Singapore Growth Triangle and the West–East Corridor across Vietnam, Laos, Cambodia, Thailand and Myanmar. We encourage contact and co-ordination among the different frameworks as well as among the relevant regional organizations in order to benefit from their best practices.

5. We shall continue to expand and deepen our linkages with the rest of the world, particularly with China, Japan and the Republic of Korea within the ASEAN + 3 framework, and with the other Dialogue Partners of ASEAN.

6. We are determined, for these purposes, to mobilize resources in partnership with other Dialogue Partners, the international community including the private sector to develop the following priority areas:

Infrastructure

7. We shall strengthen our transportation linkages through developing and implementing more extensive land, sea and air infrastructural projects in order to facilitate the flow of goods

and people and to generate higher income for people in the region. Such projects include the Singapore–Kunming Rail Link and the ASEAN Highway Network, We urge the international community to provide technical support to and participate in these major infrastructural projects.

8. We look forward to the expeditious implementation of the trans-ASEAN energy networks consisting of the ASEAN Power Grid and the trans-ASEAN Gas Pipeline projects; which would help ensure the security and sustainability of energy supplies in ASEAN.

Human Resource Development

9. We place the highest priority on the development of human resources as the key to economic growth, social stability and human fulfilment.

10. We are encouraged by the assistance being extended by ASEAN Member Countries to the newer Member Countries in various areas of human resource development including under the IAI framework.

11. We attach greet importance to the establishment and strengthening of training institutes and programmes in CLMV and their linkage with those in the other ASEAN Member Countries *for* mutual assistance.

12. We strongly encourage efforts to promote and upgrade the Use of English as a tool of communication among all peoples of ASEAN in order to make ASEAN competitive in the knowledge-based economy.

13. We recognize the need to explore the setting up of benchmarks and time-tables in the field of education to ensure the development of skills and attitudes of our people required by the knowledge-based economy and the information age.

14. We welcome the comprehensive assessment being undertaken of the training needs of government officials in CLMV, and urge international support to meet these training needs while mobilizing our own resources for this endeavour.

Information and Communication Technology

15. ASEAN is determined to use information and communication technology (ICT) as a tool for narrowing the development gap

and closing the digital divide within and among Member Countries as well as between ASEAN and the rest of the world. We reaffirm the importance for ASEAN to promote the development and the use or ICT for raising people's income, especially in the rural areas, for improving the system of public education, and for enhancing the benefits of public health and medical care for the poor. Therefore, we call for the urgent implementation of the e-ASEAN Framework Agreement and the Asian IT Belt initiative.

16. We look forward to the expeditious liberalization and facilitation of trade and investment in the ICT sector to ensure the widespread availability and use of inexpensive ICT goods and services, and to adopt concrete measures aimed at facilitating e-commerce in the region.

17. We reaffirm the importance of the assessment to be conducted, with international support, of the needs of CLMV in terms of their e-readiness, especially the level of ICT skills and infrastructure requirements. We call on the international community including the private sector to co-operate with ASEAN in meeting those needs effectively.

Regional Economic Integration

18. We fully support the measures being undertaken to integrate CLMV into ASEAN as a regional economy, including the ASEAN Free Trade Area, the ASEAN Investment Area and liberalization of trade in services.

19. We especially welcome the decision by the ASEAN Economic Ministers on the extension of unilateral preferential treatment by the six older ASEAN Member Countries to imports from CLMV on bilateral basis.

20. We call for renewed resolve to conclude the remaining protocols necessary to implement the ASEAN Agreement on Goods in Transit so as to facilitate land transport in Southeast Asia and lower its cost. We look forward to the early conclusion of the ASEAN multi-modal and inter-state transport agreements.

21. We reaffirm the importance of expanding more efficient air services in our region for the freer movement of people and goods. This would greatly help integrate the ASEAN region, foster commercial and human contacts, and stimulate broad-based economic activities and growth. In this light, we reiterate ASEAN's

resolve to develop a Competitive Air Services Policy which may be a gradual step toward an Open Sky Policy in ASEAN.

22. We reiterate the call of our Governments on members of the World Trade Organization (WTO) to expedite the accession of Cambodia, Laos and Vietnam to the Organization so as to enable them to benefit more fully from the multilateral trading system in the world market.

23. We shall step up our efforts to make possible the participation of Cambodia, Laos and Myanmar in the working groups of APEC and ASEM with a view to their eventual full membership in those forums.

24. We shall convene a workshop in Cambodia to develop a comprehensive and coherent programme for the Mekong development co-operation, especially for the integration of CLMV into the ASEAN economic mainstream. We likewise support the convening of a seminar in Brunei Darussalam on "Complementing Regional Integration through Sub-regional Groupings/Growth Areas such as the BIMP–EAGA, IMS–GT, IMT–GT and the Greater Mekong Sub-region".

25. We shall establish an IAI Unit in the ASEAN Secretariat to enhance its capability in co-ordinating and supporting ASEAN's efforts in realizing the objectives of this Declaration.

ADOPTED in Hanoi on 23 July 2001

5

Japan's Role in ASEAN-10 Under Globalization: A Japanese Perspective

Ryokichi Hirono

1. Introduction

During the last three decades leading up to mid-1990s, ASEAN countries have in general recorded sustained economic growth while undergoing fundamental changes in terms of per capita income, economic structure, foreign trade composition and foreign capital participation. They have also made an enormous progress in the social dimensions of development as expressed in longevity, literacy, school enrolment and poverty reduction. Political reforms have also followed these economic and social achievements, enabling in a varying degree among its member countries to move further to multi-party system, people's participation in national and community decision-making processes and smooth changes in political leadership.

Two extraordinary events have taken place since the mid-1990s. One was the enlargement of the ASEAN-6 consisting of Brunei, Indonesia, Malaysia, Philippines, Singapore and Thailand to the ASEAN-10, bringing into the family Cambodia, Laos PDR, Myanmar and the Socialist Republic of Vietnam. While these newcomers to ASEAN have contributed to the enlargement of the ASEAN market and the strengthening of the ASEAN's bargaining position vis-à-vis the rest of the world, they have also brought in a series of new problems that ASEAN has had to grapple with. These include among others the need for adjustments in intra-ASEAN trade, tariffs and investment rules, establishing mechanisms for narrowing the gap between the ASEAN-6 and the new ASEAN-4 and reformulating ASEAN's collective positions vis-à-vis the rest of the world in the light of the new ASEAN-4 having been under the socialist political regime in transition to market-oriented economies.

The other was the painful experience of the Asian Financial Crisis of 1997–98 and the consequent negative economic growth which all of a sudden the ASEAN countries had to go through, with lingering effects still felt today. It has been argued that behind the abrupt changes in the course of economic development of the ASEAN countries since the mid-1990s lay the increasing pressures of economic globalization both promoted by the World Trade Organisation (WTO), successor to the General Agreement on Tariffs and Trade (GATT) in 1994 and assisted by International Monetary Fund (IMF) and the World Bank and the inability of these countries to adjust to the relentless challenges of globalization particularly in the financial sectors.

This joint study 2002–2003 has followed our preliminary study 2000–2001 which in the main had analyzed both the major development performance, issues and policies in the original ASEAN-5 countries during the last four decades including the painful experiences of the Asian Financial Crisis of 1997–98 and its aftermath and the role of external assistance and in particular Japanese official development assistance (ODA) in their development process from both Japanese and ASEAN perspectives.[1]

The new joint study has attempted to review what domestic reforms have so far been effectively introduced in these ASEAN-5 countries as a result of the Asian Financial Crisis and what more to be done to accelerate and consolidate such reforms at home on one hand and, given the new ASEAN-4, to strengthen both intra- and extra-ASEAN regional co-operation framework on the other. Through these domestic reforms the ASEAN-10 countries will hopefully be able during the first decade or two of the 21st century both, to make a smooth economic and social transformation under the increasing pressures of globalization and to accommodate the two highly competitive giant economies of Asia, China and India, which are now partners under WTO's regime. The study has also sought to identify what could be the role of Japan in promoting its economic relations with the ASEAN-10 countries under the ongoing framework of the WTO and the ASEAN + 3 in the first few decades of the new century in the light of the current trend toward greater regionalism seen in Europe and the Americas that should hopefully be consistent with the WTO regime.

2. Advance of Globalization and its Economic Implications to the Old and Original ASEAN-5 and the New ASEAN-4 as Late-comers

In the analysis of the ASEAN-5 development experiences during the last four decades or so, a late-comer hypothesis has been advanced.

The hypothesis which is intended to explain most of the policy developments in the ASEAN-5 countries during the post-war period runs as follows.

The ASEAN-5 countries (and, for that matter, the ASEAN-6 and the ASEAN-10) have come into the international economic and political scene rather late as compared to Japan, North America and West European countries. The ASEAN-10 countries, except for Thailand, were all colonized by Western countries for centuries before their political independence in the immediate post-war period. In their struggle to gain national identity and catch-up with their forerunners in the international community, the governments and political leadership of these ASEAN countries had to mobilize all the essential resources, i.e., human, financial, technological and institutional, available at home and abroad to quicken their pace of economic development. During the Cold War era, the ASEAN-5 countries as late-comer market economies were able to impose on their own people economic, political and social discipline and, in spite of such domestic policies, obtained from the West adequate financial and technological resources through trade, investment and aid, following the typical developmental market-economy approach, unlike early-comer western countries which had followed more or less a liberal market-economy approach.[2] In contrast, the new ASEAN-4 countries in the continental Southeast Asia as late-comers followed a central planned economy approach similar to China, while obtaining foreign assistance mainly from the Communist bloc.

The original ASEAN-5 countries as newly independent late-comers were able to learn from both positive and negative lessons of the development experiences of early-comers such as Japan, North American and Western European countries. Throughout the last four decades 1960–1990s they have tried to integrate themselves into the world economy through open-door policies which promoted rapid trade expansion, mobilized financial, technological and managerial resources from overseas and enabled an access to lucrative industry country markets through closer linkages with multinational corporations (MNCs) based in advanced industrial countries. They also did their best not to repeat the same mistakes experienced by the industrial countries in formulating and implementing macroeconomic and microeconomic policy measures in their early stage of development. In other words, the ASEAN-5 countries succeeded at a varying degree in their development process in obtaining the late-comer benefits at home.[3]

Also, under the Cold War regime, the West was willing to provide the ASEAN-5 and, for that matter, all market-friendly developing countries with a number of trade and other economic concessions such as the infant industry protection, local contents requirements and the Generalised System of Preferences (GSP) under the GATT. There was a steady flow of concessionary financial resources and technical assistance from bilateral and multilateral sources to these ASEAN economies, particularly from Japan and the Bretton Woods institutions. Generally speaking, the West even condoned the authoritarian regimes and at times accommodated the political dictatorship in developing countries as long as the latter were anti-communist.[4]

In summary, the ASEAN-5 countries as late-comers tried to maximize the positive lessons of early-comers and minimize their negative lessons had been successful at least up until the end of 1980s under the Cold War regime in mobilizing essential human, financial and technological resources at home and abroad under favourable terms from the international community, without concomitant reforms of economic, political and social policies and institutions at home. The ASEAN-5 countries had thus been able to take advantage of late-comer benefits both at home and in the international setting.

The pressures of economic globalization, with the installation of the Reaganomics and the Thatcherism in the early 1980s, heightened its tempo and fervour, resulting in the IMF and the World Bank to pursue their Structural Adjustment Programmes (SAPs) in their borrowing developing countries with such economic conditionalities as domestic de-regulation, competition policy, foreign trade and exchange liberalization, lean government and the privatization of state-owned enterprises. The ongoing process of economic globalization, with the collapse of the Soviet Union, further took a sharp turn into bilateral and multilateral pressures of political globalization, resulting in these Bretton Woods institutions introducing in their respective short-term and long-term lending programmes political conditionalities of party pluralism, governance, transparency, accountability and participation of the civil society.

No longer in the post-Cold War regime of the 1990s developing countries including the ASEAN-6 could engage in their traditional strategies of sustained economic growth and development simply by maximizing the mobilization of internal and external resources while simultaneously obtaining trade and other economic concessions from the international community without concomitant reforms of economic, political and social policies and institutions at home. In other words, since the beginning of the 1990s the ASEAN-5 countries could no longer gain the late-comer benefits alone without paying the late-comer costs.[5]

The new era after the collapse of the Soviet Union demanded the ASEAN-5 countries to install and consolidate internal economic, political and social discipline consistent with the trade, investment and financial liberalization along the Washington Consensus and Good Governance. In spite of such radical changes in the international economic policies of major Western countries and the Bretton Woods institutions emanating from the end of the Cold War regime, the ASEAN-5 countries, probably with the exception of Singapore, continued to assume the late-comer benefits to accrue to them. Unfortunately they did not prepare themselves soon enough and effectively enough to confront the late-comer costs and undergo all the essential policy and institutional reforms required in their economic, political and social spheres.

These domestic reforms would have been essential if these ASEAN countries had aspired to sustain a continued economic growth while simultaneously reducing, if not eliminating, the late-comer costs, i.e., those policy distortions, vested interests and institutional rigidities caused and accumulated over time as a result of the continued high growth at the expense of economic, social, political and environmental equity. Had these ASEAN countries been aware of the late-comer costs and ready to take early action in their domestic policies and institutional reforms particularly in the financial sector, the Asian Financial Crisis would not have been so serious and so devastating as it had been. Similar observations can be made in the case of Hong Kong, the Republic of Korea, and Taipei, China.[6]

ASEAN as an sub-regional co-operation mechanism among its member states has had a long history of intra-ASEAN co-operation, reflecting both successes and failures, at times even generating some suspicion that it would fade away soon. It is understood in this connection that ASEAN and for that matter any regional and sub-regional co-operation mechanisms, being an instrument of promoting their member states' economic and social development and possibly political wellbeing, should be considered as successful if the mechanisms or institutions have contributed to achieving these objectives for which they are created. Also, it seems inevitable that these benefits accruing from such co-operation would differ among member states, depending upon differences in their respective capacities of utilizing such mechanism/institutions to their benefit. ASEAN is no exception to this, resulting in Singapore having benefited more than any other member states.[7]

With the entry of the New ASEAN + 4 into the enlarged ASEAN in the mid-1990s and the Asian Financial Crisis of 1997–98, many changes have taken place within ASEAN and its external arrangements since the late 1990s, most outstanding of which are the realignment of the ASEAN Free Trade Area (AFTA) arrangements, bilateral free trade agreements by individual ASEAN countries, the intra-ASEAN + 3 (APT) currency swapping scheme, the creation of the ASEAN bond market as agreed upon in the Chiang Mai Initiative and the assistance by the Old ASEAN-6 to the New ASEAN-4 to close the wide gaps and in some cases the widening ones between the old and the new members of the ASEAN.

The old AFTA agreed upon at the Bandung Summit eliminating intra-ASEAN tariff barriers by 2005 has been realigned at the Kuala Lumpur, Manila and other ASEAN Summits to take into account the adverse impact of the Asian Financial Crisis and the weaker economies of the new members of continental Southeast Asia. These events gave a breathing space to the latter in liberalizing their intra- and extra-ASEAN tariff and non-tariff barriers, as amply discussed by the ASEAN colleagues participating in this joint study. There have also been a number of initiatives taken by the Old ASEAN-6 to assist the New ASEAN-4 to accelerate the latter's economic and social development and close the gap. Japan has been collaborating with these efforts by ASEAN countries, as shown in the Japan–Singapore Partnership Programme and the Japan–Thailand Partnership Programme under which Japan and these ASEAN countries have joined together in assisting Cambodia, Laos PDR and Vietnam.[8]

Furthermore, in the late 1990s and the first decade of the 21st century, there have emerged three major changes in the external economic and political environments facing the ASEAN-10. One is the challenge of China's continuing economic growth and its more "self-confident" economic policy toward the ASEAN, its Asian neighbours and even the rest of the world. To deal with this, ASEAN went ahead in November 2002 in Phnom Penh to sign with China the Framework Agreement on Comprehensive Economic Co-operation between ASEAN and China, aiming to conclude ASEAN–China Free Trade Area by 2012.

The second is the implications of not only India's emergence as a major economic power in Asia and the Pacific area but its more "self-assertive" economic policy toward the countries of South Asia and the ASEAN. To deal with this new issue more comprehensively, ASEAN has long invited India to sit as an observer in the ASEAN Post-Ministerial Conference (ASEAN–PMC) created in 1978 and also participate fully in the ASEAN Regional Forum (ARF), which was established in 1990, to maintain peace and security in Asia. Furthermore, both the first and the second challenges have given an impetus to the concept of the East Asian Economic Community as proposed and recommended by the East Asia Study Group to the APT Summit in Phnom Penh in Cambodia last November, 2002.

Third, with the growing political instability in the Korean Peninsula emanating from the Democratic People's Republic of Korea (North Korea) armed with the threat of nuclear programmes developing into a mass-destructive weapon arsenal, ASEAN invited North Korea to participate in ARF discussion, followed up by the most recent meeting of the ASEAN–Europe Meeting (ASEM), installed in 1996, in Dalian in July, 2003 which appealed to North Korea to cease any course of action which might threaten the peace and security of the Korean Peninsula, the whole East Asia and the rest of the world. The meeting also appealed to the co-operation of all governments concerned to make the Peninsula a nuclear-free zone, as proclaimed by ASEAN in the past.

Under these rapidly changing circumstances in Asia, Japan's concern with its relations with the ASEAN has had no choice but to increasingly reorient its regional foreign policy toward assisting the ASEAN countries to deal more effectively and on an accelerated tempo both with their internal late-comer costs mentioned above, and with the possible impact of the two regional economic giants upon their respective economies, thus focussing on their ramifications to Japan–ASEAN relations in the first decade or two of the 21st century and on the possible impact of North Korean nuclear threat upon the peace and stability in Northeast Asia and the larger Asian region. These issues have now been placed on the official agenda of meetings of both ASEAN + 3 Summit in Phnom Penh in November 2002 and ASEM in Dalian in July 2003 for the first two regional issues and at the G8 Summit at Evian in July, 2003 for the third issue.

3. The Role of Japan in the ASEAN and East Asia

Japan, realizing its GDP constituting nearly one half of the combined GDP of East Asia, has fully recognized its regional responsibility in maintaining sustained economic growth, promoting industrial restructuring through technological development and transfer, improving the quality of life of all people, and ensuring peace and security in the region. It is for this reason that in spite of a long period of economic recession, Japan has been constantly liberalizing its trading and investment regimes and until recently expanding its official development assistance (ODA), maintaining until last year its position of the Number One ODA provider among the OECD/DAC countries. While some protectionist sentiment is rising among farmers and some segments of the small- and medium-industrial sectors who are facing intense competition with foreign suppliers, the government of Japan has in the main adhered to the WTO's open trading regime not only for the benefit of the Japanese consumers but also for the benefit of developing countries.

Japan has also been negotiating a number of bilateral investment agreements with Asian and other developing countries in the hope that such agreements would facilitate foreign direct investment by Japanese multinational corporations which have been choosy in investing overseas for their own survival under increasing global competition. In the recent Cabinet decision of new ODA Charter, Japan intends to maintain its ODA priority in Asia, particularly in ASEAN, as in the past three decades or so, but reorient its ODA priority in favour of conflict prevention/ resolution and post-conflict rehabilitation and reconstruction as well as in social sectors such as health, education and environment, though its ODA flows to physical infrastructure will probably continue to be important at least in the first decade of the 21st century.

For a long time there has been a keen interest in Japan for closer economic relations and co-operation in Asia, particularly with ASEAN countries and others in East Asia. This author has been an ardent proponent for ASEAN Economic Community and East Asian Economic Co-operation/Community since the mid-1970s where to sustain economic growth with social equity the centrality of domestic economics, social and political reforms in all its possible member-countries, coupled with expanded economic co-operation at the regional level has been emphasized against the backdrop of global peace and stability.[9] In the early days, the government of Japan welcomed any loose mechanisms for promoting regional co-operation such as ECAFE, the predecessor to ESCAP, Asian Highway Programme, Asian and Pacific Development Centre (APDC) and others. Later with a surging interest in Asian developing countries in further deepening regional co-operation, the GOJ became more forward-looking in strengthening such mechanism, as long as it involved the United States and other industrial countries around the Pacific such as Australia, Canada and New Zealand.

This hesitation on the part of the GOJ reflected essentially two concerns they had held for long. One was, as shown in the establishment of Asia–Pacific Economic Co-operation (APEC) in 1989, to engage the U.S. in any collective efforts, whether for economic or security co-operation in Asia so that such efforts would not be construed by the rest of Asia as a re-assertion of Japan's predominance against the historical legacy of the World War II. Though Japan was a driving force for initiating APEC, its inauguration assembly was convened by the Government of Australia to avoid any suspicion about Japan on the part of ASEAN and other developing Asian countries. Another was their "unwarranted" concern with shouldering the "burden" of economic co-operation, particularly ODA and other development financing by Japan alone, in spite of the positive image to be created for Japan among Asian partner countries. It was the initiative of Japan to establish the Asian Development Bank (ADB) in 1966, following the first meeting convened in Tokyo in the same year of the Ministerial Conference for Economic Development of Southeast Asia, but Japan went ahead in sharing the top capital subscription equally with the U.S. and invited European partners in funding the ADB.

In recent years Japan has responded positively to Asia–European co-operation by joining the ASEM in spite of the absence of U.S. participation, an indication of Japan's growing interest in working closely not only with the U.S. but also with the European Union whose geopolitical and economic importance have been growing with the enlargement of EU expected in 2004. As long as the coverage of countries for closer economic co-operation is concerned, the GOJ's priority has always been given to countries of ASEAN and East Asia, though noting as mentioned earlier a closer collaboration of ASEAN with India both at its ASEAN–PMC and the ARF.

There has been a sea-change in Japan's foreign economic policy in recent years. For several decades since the 1960s' Japan has pursued to deepen its bilateral economic relations with each and every country of the Old ASEAN-6 and the New ASEAN-4, and for that matter with every Asian country. While still retaining its keen interest to have closer bilateral economic and political relations, Japan has become keenly aware of the increasing importance of regional and sub-regional co-operation not only as a positive step toward WTO-consistent freer global trading regime, but also to cement regional and sub-regional economic and political solidarity in the face of the ever expanding European Union and similar trends in the Americas.

In order to strengthen the bargaining position of Japan vis-à-vis the EU and North American Free Trade Area (NAFTA), whether in economic or political arena, Japan needs its Asian neighbours and their solid support. This would be rather difficult simply by maintaining Japan's traditional approach of deeper bilateral relations. Hence, a keen and growing interest of Japan in recent years in enhancing its regional economic and political co-operation with its ASEAN and Asian neighbours. This changing foreign policy approach coincides with an inevitable interest among the Old ASEAN-6 to assist its New ASEAN-4 through regional co-operation in closing the widening gaps between the two in an effort to strengthen their ASEAN solidarity on one hand, and with a keen interest among the ASEAN to deal with the rising tide of China and the Republic of Korea in co-operation with Japan, while counteracting against the overwhelming Japan in co-operation with China and the Republic of Korea.[10]

The proposal made by the Prime Minister Koizumi of Japan last November in Phnom Penh at the Summit of the ASEAN + 3 for the Japan–ASEAN Comprehensive Economic Partnership, the conclusion of a bilateral Japan–Singapore Economic Partnership Agreement and the Japan's negotiation now going on with the Republic of Korea, Thailand, Malaysia and the Philippines for bilateral economic partnerships can all be interpreted as Japan's response to these changes in the regional economic scene precipitated by the emerging economic giants of China and India. Japan's increasingly serious involvement in the discussion of the ARF where both China, India and North Korea are participating can be also interpreted as exemplifying Japan's keen interest in maintaining peace and security in the ASEAN and the greater Asian region through regional co-operation. Under these economic and political circumstances Japan can no longer expect to sit still in the back seat and to be solely concerned with enhancing its economic relations with the ASEAN through trade, investment and aid as she had done from the '60s to the '80s.[11]

Japan and its ASEAN and other Asian neighbours now realize it to be Japan's regional and global responsibility under globalization to contribute to ensuring the collective economic prosperity, sustainable development and peace and security at the regional level in partnership with its neighbours in Asia and at the global level in partnership with the rest of the industrial and developing worlds. These emerging responsibilities of Japan as perceived by its Asian neighbours and the rest, however, require above all the continued process of domestic economic, social and political reforms, as it does in each and every ASEAN and East Asian country, which will contribute to sustained economic growth, improved quality of life and environment not only in Japan but in the neighbouring ASEAN and Asia as well as in the rest of the world. Japan therefore must carry out these painful but essential domestic reforms not only for its own survival under an increasing tempo of globalization, but also for the benefit of its ASEAN and Asian neighbours and the global community.[12]

It is for these fundamental reasons that the current study looks at: 1) major economic, trade and investment policy and institutional reforms in the ASEAN-5 since the crisis; 2) implications of the new ASEAN-4 to the intra-ASEAN economic co-operation framework; 3) possible impact of the continuing economic growth and "self-assertive" foreign economic policies of China and India on the ASEAN-5; and 4) reorienting Japanese policy toward the ASEAN-10 under increasing pressures of economic and political globalization to seize a golden opportunity for initiating East Asian Comprehensive Economic Partnership and East Asian economic Co-operation Conference as an inevitable follow-up process from the ongoing ASEAN + 3 framework. It is to be noted in this connection, however, that Japan must compete neither with China nor the Republic of Korea in forging the economic alliance in East Asia, but work in collaboration with these two countries for the benefit of ASEAN and all the countries in the region.

In closing, the author wishes to express his great pleasure to have had an opportunity to work with his colleagues in the five ASEAN countries during the last year on this joint study project, and share the common objective of exploring into the possibility of forging a new dynamism of regional co-operation in East Asia to ensure sustained economic growth, improved quality of life, cleaner environment, and peace and security in the region. The author also wishes to express his sincere thanks to all the study participants from the five ASEAN countries:

Indonesia: Dr. Hadi Soesastro, CSIS, Jakarta; Malaysia: Dr. Stephen Leong, Assistant DG, ISIS, Kuala Lumpur; Philippines: Dr. Gwendolyn R. Tecson, Professor, UP, Quezon; Singapore: Dr. Hank Lim, Director, Singapore Institute of International Affairs; Thailand: Dr. Deunden Nikomborirak, Senior Research Fellow and Dr. Somkiat Tangkitvanich, Research Fellow, TDRI, Bangkok.

Notes

[1] Hirono, Ryokichi (ed.) (2001), ASEAN no Taigai Kankei ni okeru ODA no Igi (Significance of Official Development Assistance in the External Relations of the ASEAN), Tokyo: Japan Institute of International Affairs (JIIA).

[2] Hirono, Ryokichi. "More Interdepencence, More Diversity: Trends and Issues in Trilateral Relations with Centrally Planned and Third World Countries". In *Trilateral Commission (1981), Trilateral Countries in the International Economy of the 1980s*, New York: Trilateral Commission, and Hirono, Ryokichi. 1996. "Sustaining Rapid Economic Development Through Industrialisation in East Asia: Japanese Approach". Japan Review, vol. 10, No. 4 (Winter, 1996) Tokyo: JIIA.

[3] Chng, Meng Kng and Ryokichi Hirono (eds.) (1984), ASEAN–Japan Industrial Cooperation: An Overview. Singapore: ISEAS, and Ng, C.Y. R. Hirono and Robert Y. Siy, Jr. (eds.) (1986), Effective Mechanism for the Enhancement of Technology and Skills in ASEAN. Singapore: ISEAS.

[4] Committee for Economic Development (CED) and Keizai Doyukai (1970), Development Assistance to Southeast Asia, New York: CED, and Blaker, Michael (ed.) (1984), Development Assistance to Southeast Asia: the U.S. and Japanese Approaches. New York: Columbia University.

[5] Hirono, Ryokichi. "Globalization and Competitiveness in the XXI Century: A Japanese Perspective," in Emmerij, Louis (ed.) (1997), Economic and Social Development into the XXI Century. Washington, D.C.: Inter-American Development Bank.

[6] Hunter, W.C., G.G. Kaufman and T. H. Krueger. 1999. The Asian Financial Crisis: Origins, Implications and Solutions, Boston: Kluwer Academic Publishers, and Hirono, Ryokichi (2001), "Globalization in the 21st Century: Blessing or Threat to Developing Countries," Asia-Pacific Review, vol. 8, No. 2, November, 2001, Tokyo: Institute of International Policy Studies.

[7] Hirono, Ryokichi. 1979. "Towards Increased Intra-ASEAN Economic Co-operation," Asia-Pacific Community: A Quarterly Review, February, and Suh, Jang-Won & Jae-Bong Ro (1990), Asia-Pacific Economic Co-operation: The Way Ahead. Seoul: Korean Institute for International Economic Policy (KIIEP).

[8] Ministry of Foreign Affairs. 2003. Waga Kuni no Seifu Kaihatsu Enjo (Japan's ODA) 2003. Tokyo: Association for Promotion of International Co-operation (APIC).

[9] Hirono, Ryokichi. 2001. Nihon no ODA Seisaku no Tenkai: Hanseiki no Sogo Hyouka no Ichi Shiron (Historical Development of Japan's ODA Policies: A Trial of ODA Policy Evaluation during the Last Half a Century). Toshi Mondai Kenkyu (Studies on Urban Issues), Vol. 53, No. 10, October, 2001.

[10] As member of the Cabinet Secretariat's advisory group, the author has consistently proposed to the GOJ since the early 1980s the necessity of organizing institutional mechanisms for closer economic relations and co-operation among developing East Asian countries covering both trade, investment and ODA as well as environment and security. It was only at the time of former Prime Minister Hashimoto when the GOJ took a leap forward by proposing to initiate the summit meetings of the ASEAN + 3 (China, Japan and ROK). For detailed discussion of this issue, please see a series of annual reports with policy recommendations by the Asia–Pacific Study Group submitted to the Cabinet Secretariat since the early 1980s. Also see the International Forum of Japan (2003), Higashi Ajia Keizai Kyodotai Koso to Nihon no Yakuwari (Toward East Asian Economic Community and the Role of Japan). Tokyo: IFJ, June, 2003 in whose discussion the author had participated.

[11] Hirono, Ryokichi. 2002. "Economic Growth and Restructuring in Postwar Japan – Contributions of Industrial and Technology Policies." In Wong, Poh-Kam and Chee-Yuen Ng (eds.), Industrial Policy, Innovation and Economic Growth: The Experiences of Japan and the Asian NIES. Singapore: Singapore University Press, and Hirono, Ryokichi. 2002. Japan's Capacity Development in the Postwar Period: Changing Roles of Government and Private Sector in the Era of Globalisation. A lecture at the JICA Young Scholars Seminar organised by Japan International Co-operation Agency (JICA) on 10 July.

[12] Before and after the proposal by Prime Minister Koizumi on Japan–ASEAN Comprehensive Economic Partnership (CEP), there have been a number of meetings where both business, academia, bureaucracy and policymakers of Japan have been discussing with counterparts of ASEAN, China and ROK on pros and cons of bilateral vs multilateral free trading arrangements/comprehensive economic partnerships. Foreign participants have been under impression that GOJ is now promoting both bilateral and multilateral CEPs and expressing their anxiety over this pluralistic approach as presenting some confusion and delays among ASEAN in actually forging closer economic partnership in East Asia, as each ASEAN partner wishes to get a better deal in their respective negotiation with Japan for bilateral CEP.